New Directions for
Higher Education

Martin Kramer
EDITOR-IN-CHIEF

D1552775

Organizational Learning in Higher Education

Adrianna Kezar
EDITOR

Number 131 • Fall 2005
Jossey-Bass
San Francisco

ORGANIZATIONAL LEARNING IN HIGHER EDUCATION
Adrianna Kezar (ed.)
New Directions for Higher Education, no. 131
Martin Kramer, Editor-in-Chief

Microfilm copies of issues and articles are available in 16mm and 35mm, as well as microfiche in 105mm, through University Microfilms Inc., 300 North Zeeb Road, Ann Arbor, Michigan 48106-1346.

NEW DIRECTIONS FOR HIGHER EDUCATION (ISSN 0271-0560, electronic ISSN 1536-0741) is part of The Jossey-Bass Higher and Adult Education Series and is published quarterly by Wiley Subscription Services, Inc., A Wiley Company, at Jossey-Bass, 989 Market Street, San Francisco, California 94103-1741. Periodicals Postage Paid at San Francisco, California, and at additional mailing offices. POSTMASTER: Send address changes to New Directions for Higher Education, Jossey-Bass, 989 Market Street, San Francisco, California 94103-1741.

New Directions for Higher Education is indexed in Current Index to Journals in Education (ERIC); Higher Education Abstracts.

SUBSCRIPTIONS cost $80 for individuals and $170 for institutions, agencies, and libraries. See ordering information page at end of journal.

EDITORIAL CORRESPONDENCE should be sent to the Editor-in-Chief, Martin Kramer, 2807 Shasta Road, Berkeley, California 94708-2011.

Cover photograph © Digital Vision

www.josseybass.com

Contents

EDITOR'S NOTES

The concept of organizational learning and learning organizations has become commonplace in the world of business and industry. In the past decade, the learning organization has been one of the most written about topics in organizational studies, and as Argyris and Schön (1996) note, it has become conventional wisdom that organizations "need to adapt to changing environments, draw lessons from past successes and failures, and detect and correct errors of the past, anticipate and respond to impending threats, engage in continuous innovation, and build and realize images of a desirable future" (p. xvii). This shift is attributable to an awareness that organizations face a host of changes, such as shifting demographics, technology innovations, and increased competition. As the need for organizational change became more apparent, individuals realized that moving beyond the status quo or current state would require learning. Peter Senge's book *The Fifth Discipline* (1990) popularized the importance of learning to organizational development, change, and performance, but the concept of learning within organizations had been studied for forty years with the work of scholars such as Cyert and March (1963) and Argyris and Schön (1978).

Although this concept has become commonplace in many organizations, higher education institutions have been less likely to apply these important concepts to their organizational functioning. It seems particularly ironic that organizations whose mission is learning have not examined the implications of learning for organizational functioning. Yet many people cite the need for learning in higher education. The most noted reason for campuses to learn is to be responsive to environmental needs and pressures such as dwindling resources. The second most noted reason is the problems plaguing higher education such as large attrition rates or rising costs as well as the challenges facing higher education such as technology or diversity. Third, commentators suggest that higher education does not learn from mistakes, such as buying the newest software before the bugs are worked out, costing the institutions thousands of dollars, or not documenting sexual assaults and having perpetrators strike again. In addition, organizational learning is considered particularly important within large, complex systems. Individuals move in and out of these systems through attrition and promotion. Learning within departments or units is particularly important for the organization to succeed. Because most higher education institutions are large, complex systems, organizational learning seems important for its continued success.

Some core debates in organizational learning are explored in this volume, with specific focus on how these concepts emerge within the higher education context. For example, some scholars believe that only individuals, not organizations, can learn. Argyris and Schön (1996) refer to the way that people typically speak of the marketing department when they realize that sales are about to decline or the administration that learned to consult the faculty before announcing a reorganization as examples of the way we commonly refer to organizational learning. There remains active debate about whether this is an interrelated process between the individual and group level or whether the group level can have independent thought and learning.

Another active debate is how organizational learning is defined and what constitutes learning. Some scholars argue that behavioral change is necessary to demonstrate learning, others insist that new ways of thinking are enough, and still others examine the potential for change or new practices (Garvin, 1993; Huber, 1991). Garvin suggests that learning cannot be said to have occurred unless there is evidence of change in the way work gets done. The chapters in this volume examine higher education scholars' views on these important debates and relate how they emerge uniquely (if they do) within the higher education context.

The volume also focuses on strategies or approaches for creating learning in higher education. The organizational learning literature explores whether a separate unit needs to be established to foster learning. In higher education, this is often the institutional research office, planning office, or Total Quality Management or change office. There is also literature on whether learning occurs through routine processes or whether certain techniques or tools need to be established, such as cross-functional teams. Some tools or mechanisms that have been developed within higher education institutions are reviewed in the volume, such as the Equity Scorecard, community service learning, and faculty development. In addition, the role of leaders (from presidents to faculty developers to institutional researchers) in fostering organizational learning is explored.

Overview

Chapter One, by Adrianna Kezar, defines terms such as *organizational learning* and the *learning organization,* providing a foundation for the later chapters. She reviews the way organizational learning and the learning organization have been applied within higher education through fads such as Total Quality Management and benchmarking. She notes how learning has been conceptualized within the higher education setting as a fad, but that the promise of this concept comes from organizational learning more so than the learning organization.

The promise of organizational learning is described in Chapter Two. Georgia L. Bauman describes a project in which teams of faculty, administrators, and staff from fourteen colleges and universities engaged in organizational learning for the purposes of improving institutional performance related to inequitable educational outcomes for African American and Latino students. She demonstrates how organizational learning was promoted in the project when three conditions existed: the presence of new ideas, the cultivation of doubt in existing knowledge and practices, and the development and transfer of knowledge among institutional actors. Learning is effectively used in order to ameliorate problems in institutional performance.

In Chapter Three, Jodi L. Anderson focuses on ways that new information can be brought to increase organizational learning. She describes how learning often occurs when an organization encounters new information, and this information is most powerful when its origins are external. University and community partnerships serve to illustrate how partnerships can be a powerful tool for internal organizational learning in an engaged institution.

When we consider the promise of organizational learning for institutional performance, it is also important to think about what kind of learning is being cultivated. In Chapter Four, Kezar examines how learning has been defined in the organizational learning literature. She argues for a broader notion of knowledge that includes emotions, values, intuition, experience, and creativity rather than merely reasoning. By using a broader view of knowledge, Kezar believes, the learning developed will be more complex and better able to address challenges of higher education institutions.

In Chapter Five, John Milam reviews the role of institutional research (IR) in enabling organizational learning and proposes a new role for IR offices—knowledge management—and its role in and relationship to transformational change. He reviews new tools such as learning histories, the need for new forms of leadership, and the importance of creating a culture where mistakes are valued and dissatisfaction is recognized as part of the learning process.

Judith A. Ramaley and Barbara A. Holland describe the key role of leaders in organizational learning in Chapter Six. Research on leadership demonstrates that the behavior of leaders affects whether people engage in learning, that is, whether they see it as a priority and whether it can improve institutional operations. She discusses her experience of transforming a campus into a learning organization specifically focused on her efforts to model learning in her decision-making, planning, and vision processes.

Continuing the themes of leadership and creating a new culture, Chapter Seven, by Devorah Lieberman, reviews the role of faculty development centers in creating organizational learning. When people think of learning within organizations, they typically envision staff or faculty development carried out by human resource or faculty development offices. Instead, she focuses on how a faculty development office can help facilitate organizational, not just individual, learning. Lieberman highlights the way a centralized office has promoted ongoing learning among faculty.

In Chapter Eight, Estela Mara Bensimon reviews how the theory and processes of organizational learning can help researchers and practitioners understand and address the structural and cultural obstacles that prevent colleges and universities from producing equitable educational outcomes.

She presents such challenges as linking individual and institutional learning. Her focus is on cognitive frames and making people's views on issues such as equity more visible so that the undiscussable becomes discussable.

In Chapter Nine, Daryl G. Smith and Sharon Parker examine the way organizational learning can be applied to help campuses create better climates for diverse students. They review the use of institutional data, a conceptual framework, and use of teams as part of an evaluation process to encourage learning. They also present some of the lessons from the project, such as connecting individual and institutional learning, the importance of creating synergy between initiatives, the difficulty of obtaining appropriate data, the importance of leadership, and the connection to mission and culture.

These last two chapters provide an in-depth look at how organizational learning is being used to tackle complex problems of equity and diversity.

Cross-Chapter Themes

One of the major themes to emerge across these chapters is contradiction. Creating learning is difficult within higher education; nevertheless, certain structures or aspects of the culture enable learning and make it easier than within other organizations. Higher education institutions have rich sources of data available, savvy users of information and research, curious individuals, values that resonate with learning, and team structures in place for decision making rather than hierarchies that impede learning (noted by Smith and Parker, Bauman, Anderson, and Milam). These are all encouraging elements. Yet other conditions block progress toward learning: the decentralization of processes and authority means that duplicate efforts develop pockets of knowledge and learning that often do not come together to provide solutions (noted by Ramaley and Holland and Smith and Parker). The decentralization also means many have trouble connecting learning to the overall organization. Large institutions have turnover and loose expertise; higher education has few networks or collective work in place since collaboration is not institutionalized to capture knowledge. Learning often entails a clarity of purpose and goals that many campuses are unable to accomplish (noted by Lieberman, Ramaley and Holland, and Smith and Parker). Few faculty and staff really want to consider themselves learners or be uncomfortable by admitting they do not know the answers (noted by Lieberman, Bensimon, and Milam) or really want to make decisions based on evidence rather than experience (noted by Bensimon and Lieberman). Learning is enabled by ideas from outside that often challenge prevailing notions and make the organization doubt current operations. Many higher education institutions are insulated from direct external influences (noted by Anderson and Bauman). Leaders need to consider what enablers and what inhibitors exist on their campus and work to mitigate the problems and build on assets.

Another theme is the importance of learning for change. Almost every chapter author, both researchers and practitioners, came to believe in organizational learning as a pivotal ingredient to change. Bensimon, Bauman, and Smith and Parker focus on the trenchant problem of creating equitable outcomes for diverse students. Anderson and Ramaley and Holland describe the need to create more external partnerships and greater involvement in community and public service. Lieberman and Ramaley and Holland review efforts to create quality learning environments. Kezar and Milam focus on the plethora of changes that face higher education from integrating technology, globalization, resource constraint, diversity, equity, and increasing partnerships. Also, organizational learning appears to be more important to facilitate complex changes that have evaded institutional problem solving for years.

Similar strategies are identified for creating learning among the various chapters. The use of cross-campus teams was found to be a key process and focal point for learning (noted by Anderson, Bauman, Bensimon, Kezar, and Smith and Parker). Teams get key people focused on an institutional priority and provide needed information to make learning occur. Also, campuses can be preemptive and set up communities of practice around key areas such as retention, engagement, or technology. When teams are brought together, there are existing networks that concentrate on campus issues. In general, working cross-functionally helps create more learning. Second, expertise in display-ing and interpreting data is another common strategy (noted by Bauman, Bensimon, Milam, and Smith and Parker). Campuses need to develop and enhance their IR functions and skills among administrators for presenting and interpreting data. Campuses need to consider displaying data in new ways and breaking routines. Third, opening up the campus to outside ideas and influences helps to promote double-looped learning, which challenges traditional assumptions (noted by Anderson, Kezar, Milam, and Ramaley and Holland). Bringing in outside speakers, consultants, partners, and others can help those on campus encounter new people and new ideas. The fact that faculty are often on the same campus for their entire career can result in their not coming into contact with new ideas about how the campus should be run. Fourth, capturing learning and making it visible builds learning Milam describes learning histories, and Lieberman and Ramaley and Holland describe the leader's role in modeling a scholarly approach to decision making and communicating learning successes. Perhaps the most important strategy is altering the culture of campuses to embrace risk taking, doubt, creativity, and discussing the undiscussable—qualities usually not characteristic of higher education institutions and that prevent learning (Bauman, Bensimon, Kezar, and Milam). Leadership is mentioned by several authors as important for creating this new culture; in particular, I direct readers to the chapters by Ramaley and Holland and Milam.

Clearly, higher education institutions have some work to do in order to foster learning. Yet the promise of projects using an organizational learning approach as well as leaders who have worked to create a culture open to learning provide direction for campuses that endeavor to steer toward a new direction rather than avoid the necessary changes. Higher education institutions should not find it surprising, given their mission of learning, that the key to their organizational success is fostering an environment of inquiry.

References

Argyris, C., and Schön, D. *Organizational Learning: A Theory of Action Perspective.* Reading, Mass.: Addison-Wesley, 1978.

Argyris, C., and Schön, D. *Organizational Learning II.* Reading, Mass.: Addison-Wesley, 1996.

Cyert, R., and March, J. *A Behavioral Theory of the Firm.* Upper Saddle River, N.J.: Prentice-Hall, 1963.

Garvin, D. "Building a Learning Organization." *Harvard Business Review,* 1993, 71(4), 78–91.

Huber, G. "Organizational Learning: The Contributing Processes and the Literature." *Organization Science,* 1991, 2(2), 88–115.

Senge, P. *The Fifth Discipline.* New York: Basic Books, 1990.

Adrianna Kezar
Editor

ADRIANNA KEZAR is associate professor at the University of Southern California in the Higher Education Administration Program.

This chapter provides an overview of the literature on organizational learning and the learning organization, sets out key concepts in each area, and reviews the way that organizational learning and the learning organization have been applied within higher education.

What Campuses Need to Know About Organizational Learning and the Learning Organization

Adrianna Kezar

On many campuses, administrators and even faculty are talking about becoming a learning organization or the importance of organizational learning. The concept of the learning organization has particularly captured the hearts of administrators. Yet these words are used in varying situations (for example, in relation to Total Quality Management, assessment, accountability, and knowledge management, to name a few) and with varying meanings. In addition to this confusion about the meaning and use of both concepts, many people on campus are concerned that the learning organization is a management fad. In their experience, fads come and go, with limited to no effectiveness or enhancement of campus operations. Other employees are concerned because learning has been discussed in relation to management fads that they distrust and have found useless, such as reengineering. Rather than ignore these valid concerns, this chapter discusses organizational learning and the learning organization as possible management fads and ways that these approaches might be engaged successfully. I describe a three-phase technique for engaging fads: exploration, implementation, and evaluation.

This chapter is mainly concerned with the first phase of exploration, in which the leader develops a clear understanding of the fad.

Is Organizational Learning a Fad in Higher Education?

Are organizational learning and the learning organizations simply another management fad that administrators and faculty should stave off?

The failure of planning programming budgeting systems, management by objectives, and zero based budgeting everywhere it was tried might have served as a cautionary tale. It could have reminded us how complicated universities are, how little we know about how they work, and how well intentioned, but misguided attempts to rationalize their affairs could lead to confusion rather than improved effectiveness. Instead we attributed our failures to lapses in leadership, institutional intransigence, and flaws in implementation. The evidence of our own experience was overwhelmed by our belief in the virtues of rationality and the legacy of the first management revolution. If one form of rationality did not work, let's try another, and another, and still another. And so we did [Birnbaum, 2000, p. 63].

This quotation from Birnbaum's *Management Fads in Higher Education* precedes a chapter about a second wave of management fads, including strategic planning, benchmarking, Total Quality Management (TQM), and business process reengineering. The concept of the learning organizations is promoted within TQM and benchmarking. Because the learning organization is a quick-fix business technique similar to other approaches that Birnbaum labels as fads, I propose it is a management fad.

Birnbaum (2000) suggests that management fads are met with initial excitement and engagement by administrators in higher education but generally not by other groups on campus. Passionate rhetoric surrounded the promotion of each management fad, which then failed to take hold or yield results or the logic of the argument began to fail among proponents swept up in yet another new management fad. Yet Birnbaum argues that even though these fads never became institutionalized to any measurable degree, each left positive and negative residuals that have changed the face of higher education over the past thirty years. He claims that the current tyranny of numbers and quantification, increasing cynicism about management, and centralization of bureaucracy are among the negative residuals; positive residuals include recognizing the importance of data, creating interaction among disparate groups and promoting new activity, and ultimately leading to a greater spirit of innovation and openness to change. Birnbaum's book is a cautionary tale based on the history of fads and advocates for the constructive use of fads.

Birnbaum (2000) offers several guidelines for "how to get the fad benefits without its potential costs, by managing academic management fads through three phases of exploration, implementation and evaluation" (p. 230). During exploration, the leader should examine the fad with skeptical interest. Most fads have kernels of wisdom, and the goal for the leader is to extract these kernels and find ways to include them within the institution without the negative residuals. During exploration, he suggests investing in knowledge and finding out as much as possible about the fad. Implementation without a proper understanding of the nuances is dangerous. Birnbaum believes a wait-and-see attitude of watching other institutions and following what has worked can be good. As leaders try to implement ideas from the fad, they will be met with resistance. They should anticipate this skepticism and respond to it by developing a cross-role exploratory committee whose members include opponents and advocates. Rather than attempt to change the entire institution at once, Birnbaum suggests pilot-testing smaller programs, demonstrating their success, and then scaling up. As the concept is being implemented, they should not overpromise the results. It is also wise to start the fad in an area where there is a high probability that it will succeed, but if it fails, the leader needs to be open to the fact that the idea may not be a good one for this campus. Being culturally sensitive and knowing the institution and how people will react to the fad are critical to implementation. Some fads fit better with certain institutional contexts. Reengineering may work better with new campuses with fewer entrenched practices and benchmarking among campuses that have clear peer groups, for example. Finally, leaders should maintain the support of the fad during experimentation and build a sound assessment plan for evaluating its performance. In the end, "academic management fads are potentially disruptive in the hands of insecure or inexperienced managers who adopt them because they do not know what else to do. Academic management fads are potentially useful when managers who have internalized the critical norms and values of their institutions add the kernel of truth in each fad to their store of knowledge and behavioral repertoire" (Birnbaum, 2000, p. 241).

Birnbaum (2000) further states that most management fads are commonsensical to most experienced managers. I suggest that the learning organization is a management fad and should be engaged with skeptical interest. The concept is also largely commonsensical, and it would be difficult for almost anyone to disagree with the importance of learning for organizational performance, especially within colleges and universities. Yet research demonstrates that there is cynicism about the concept of the learning organization within higher education. Jeris (1998) found consensus among senior administrators that the terms *organizational learning* and *learning organization* were viewed with great skepticism on campuses, particularly by faculty. Yet there was general agreement among faculty and administrators that the concepts from organizational learning made sense. Another assumption of this chapter, as well as the entire volume, is that organizational learning is perhaps a better approach to engage than the narrower concept of the learning organization, which is, by Birnbaum's definition, a fad. Leaders will be more successful if they engage concepts from organizational learning but try not to get caught up in the learning organization bandwagon.

I believe that following Birnbaum's proposed process will be the most successful way to engage universities in embracing the positive elements of learning organizations. This chapter focuses on the first step of exploration: gaining knowledge about the learning organization and organizational learning so that individuals become informed consumers and providing data on how these concepts have been used within higher education.

Getting It Straight: Organizational Learning versus the Learning Organization

Most people confuse the notions of organizational learning and the learning organization. Organizational learning is the study of whether, how, and under what conditions organizations can be said to learn (Fiol & Lyles, 1985). The concept has a long history beginning in the 1950s with researchers such as Herbert Simon. It is not a management fad but a long-term, systematic body of research (Argyris and Schön, 1996). It emerged in organizational psychology as researchers began to observe what they thought was a new phenomenon, whereby collectives could be seen to learn as a whole rather than just individually. Individual learning and organizational learning are distinctive concepts. Individuals within organizations are constantly learning, but a learning organization is an environment that promotes a culture of learning, a community of learners, and it ensures that individual learning enriches and enhances the organization as a whole. Huber (1991) offers the following definition in his review of forty years of writings: "An organizational entity learns if, through its processing of information, the range of its potential behaviors is changed and an organization learns if any of its units acquires knowledge that it recognizes as potentially useful to the organization" (p. 89).

Organizational learning, which is associated with academics, tends to be less prescriptive and is neutral with respect to the value of learning (Argyris and Schön, 1996). Learning may be either good or bad and may or may not be linked to effective action. Some scholars believe that only individuals, not organizations, can learn. There remains active debate about whether this is an interrelated process between the individual and group level or whether the group level can have independent thought and learning (Dierkes, 2001). For those who believe that learning can occur at an organizational level, many do not believe organizations currently engage in such learning, so the term is somewhat meaningless because it does not exist empirically. Some scholars argue that behavioral change is necessary, and others insist that new ways of thinking are enough (Garvin, 1993). Garvin suggests that learning cannot be said to have occurred unless there is evidence of change in the way work gets done.

Some of the main concepts in organizational learning are single- and double-looped learning, inquiry and action, theories-in-use, overload, and information interpretation processes such as unlearning and organizational memory (among many others). Single-looped learning refers to the detection of errors in alignment with the environment and finds ways to do so based on existing assumptions and values; it results in incremental change. Double-looped learning entails challenging existing assumptions and beliefs to align the institution to the environment and therefore requires transformational change. Inquiry and advocacy is a form of dialogue that helps individuals understand underlying assumptions and values that prevent people from having honest communication and sometimes also block learning (Argyris and Schön, 1996). Theories-in-use (mental models) refer to beliefs that guide action; learning occurs when new ideas are presented or doubt occurs to challenge existing theories of use. Overload refers to organizational units having more information to be interpreted than the capacity of the unit to process that information (Huber, 1991). Often organizations produce too many reports, data, and detailed information that cannot be meaningfully reviewed, and learning is less likely to occur in these situations than with more limited, targeted sets of information. Organizational memory is concerned with examining the many threats to recall, such as employee turnover, nonanticipation of future information needs, and storing of data where few people can find the information (Huber, 1991).

In addition to concepts related to learning, studies examine features within organizations found to encourage learning: decentralization (rather than hierarchy), trust between employees and managers, new information systems, incentives and rewards, learning culture, open communication, sharing of information, staff development and training, and inquiry units (such as institutional research or teams within units). Organizational learning also focuses on threats to learning (Argyris and Schön, 1996). For example, Levitt and March's studies (1988) illustrate competence traps in which organizations use strategies from the past routinely without looking at the current situation and superstitious learning in which individuals and groups draw inferences from subjective experience. Defensive reasoning, another threat to learning, is when people continue with a course of action for fear it will illustrate they were wrong in the past or fear experimenting because they may fail. Levitt and March also suggest that learning may prove inferior to other choices, such as bargaining, history-dependent decision making, rational choice, or politics. Learning has its place, but it is not always effective or efficient; for example, organizations often do not have time to collect data, learn, and make decisions.

The concept of the learning organization evolved out of the research from organizational learning and became popular in the early 1990s. Some of the key writers are Senge (1990), Schein (1985), and Garvin (1993). The learning organization emerged in response to concerns that American firms were unable to respond to challenges from the external environment and that bureaucratic structures had created inflexible, routinized environments where workers no longer engaged in thoughtful reflection. It focuses on creating organizations that can be adaptable, flexible, experimental, and innovative. Similar to organizational learning, the learning organization is a contested area where there are multiple definitions of the concept. However, most commentators consider the learning organization to be an idealized model (and a fad), and this ideal was popularized in Peter Senge's *Fifth Discipline* (1990). Generally, the learning organization is more optimistic about the possibility of organizations to learn and of the efficacy of learning for organizational effectiveness than organizational learning writers.

Learning organization writers focus on ways to overcome threats to learning rather than emphasizing the threats to learning.

Within Senge's model (1990), learning organizations use five disciplines in order to create learning: systems thinking, mental models, personal mastery, shared vision, and team learning/dialogue. Most of the disciplines represent ways to overcome threats to learning. Systems thinking is based on the notion that there is a set of causal relationships, nonlocal and complex, that can be described and can lead to awareness and learning for organizations stuck in the misguided mind-set of direct, local, and simple causal relationships (Garvin, 1993; Senge, 1990). A focus on direct, local, causal relationships results in organizations' misdiagnosing issues and prevents learning. Senge's (1990) principle of "seeing the forest and the trees" is an attempt to overcome this threat to organizational learning that often frustrates progress and makes people give up on innovations. Mental models are another core aspect of understanding learning organizations; they refer to the taken-for-granted beliefs and assumptions that people hold that can prevent learning if they are not challenged when new information or data are provided (referred to as theories-in-use by Argyris and Schön). Leaders need to use reflection skills to identify their own mental model and inquiry skills to ascertain those of others.

Personal mastery is the process of continuous learning by individuals and being open to new challenges and the creative tension of moving from the current reality of the organization to a new vision. As Senge (1990) notes, "From their quest for continual learning (through personal mastery) comes the spirit of the learning organization" (p. 141). Organizations will not learn and evolve if individuals do not make a commitment to learn and see their lives as a creative journey. Personal mastery links individual performance to organizational performance.

Shared vision refers to the ability for leaders to instill a common purpose, which provides the force and energy for learning. The last discipline is team learning, which is the process of aligning and developing the capacity of a team to create the results its members truly desire. The other four disciplines are all connected to systems thinking. Shared vision relies on systems thinking; for example, Senge (1990) argues, "Vision paints the picture of what we want to create. Systems thinking reveals how we have created what we currently have" (p. 231).

Garvin (1993), another major writer within the area of the learning organization, identifies five main activities (processes) that organizations use to become a learning organization: systematic problem solving, experimentation with new approaches, learning from experience and past history, learning from the experiences and best practices of others, and transferring knowledge quickly and efficiently throughout the organization.

Systematic problem solving is the practice of relying on the scientific method, rather than guesswork, for diagnosing problems and insisting on data rather than hunches or assumptions as background for decision making. Experimentation involves the systematic searching for and testing of new knowledge. Garvin (1993) notes that experimentation is close to systematic problem solving; it is not focused on immediate problems but anticipates future problems. He provides the example of a glass company that continually tries out new formulas to develop better grades of glass. Learning from experience is also described as a scientific process in which the organization systematically assesses its performance and uses these data to correct actions. Although systematic review of the organization's performance can create learning, Garvin also suggests that organizations can learn from others. The process of benchmarking is one of the main tools for learning from others. Through direct comparison of data between one's organizations and others, new information about ways to conduct business emerges. Knowledge transfer is another part of the learning process, and Garvin recommends reporting as a primary way to distribute learning among members of an organization.

Both organizational learning and the learning organization share some common ideas. In general, both are concerned with processes for acquiring information, interpreting data, developing knowledge, and sustaining learning. In terms of shared concepts, both focus on the importance of systems thinking and viewing the organization as a system. Mental models (theories-in-use) and challenging assumptions are critical within both bodies of work. The level at which learning occurs is also a consideration across both concepts, emphasizing that individual, group, and overall organizational learning are interactive and necessary for organizational learning to occur. Data and new ideas (through best practices or benchmarking) are helpful for creating knowledge. Experimentation and innovation are also highly encouraged within both organizational learning and the learning organization, departing from existing operating assumptions.

The primary difference in these two areas of study is the degree to which learning is seen as possible, effective, and desirable. Organizational learning focuses more on the study of threats to and limitations with organizational learning, while the learning organization focuses on the processes for overcoming threats to learning; it overpromises success, as Birnbaum notes of fads. The learning organization is a management fad, a proposed ideal state of organizational functioning; it is not based on empirical research, although the ideas embedded in it are drawn from empirical research in organizational learning. Also, the learning organization tends to focus more on external threats as the reason for fostering learning and looks for external forces and logic to prompt learning, whereas organizational learning writers discuss internal concerns for performance and learning as part of the condition of human beings within settings. Learning is a phenomenon inherent in human processes to some degree, but it is fraught with threats and complexity, leaving leaders with few easy answers about how to facilitate organizational learning.

Evolution of Organizational Learning and the Learning Organization in Higher Education

A next step down the path of exploration is to examine the way organizational learning and the learning organization have been used within higher education and determine what research within the college or university environment exists to inform implementation. Research from organizational theory suggests that techniques and practices are more easily and successfully adopted within an institution when the approach has been tested within that particular setting and adjusted for that context (Birnbaum, 1988; Eckel and Kezar, 2003). But this proves to be a difficult task. Direct and clear reference to organizational learning and the learning organization within the literature in higher education is infrequent. As Jeris (1998) notes,

> A search of the literature regarding organizational learning and learning organizations within the context of higher education yielded virtually nothing. Considerable experimentation with electronic searches was necessary to understand how these concepts are being used and to identify any research that has been conducted (mostly it is identified as part of other concepts such as total quality management, etc.) [p. 7].

In 2005, a search of several education-related databases yielded 120 references to the learning organization and 58 to organizational learning. Overwhelmingly, and perhaps not surprisingly, scholars and practitioners are writing more about the fad than the research-based tradition.

Organizational learning and *the learning organization* tend to be used interchangeably in the literature, without recognition that they are distinctive concepts. In addition, most references are vague, without clear definition or reference to concepts within either tradition. Organizational learning and the learning organization are not considered independently, but are intertwined with other concepts, such as TQM, assessment, human resource management, and knowledge management, with TQM and assessment being the main references to learning. A few writers (Alpert and Petrie, 1982; Neumann, 1988) have applied organizational learning concepts within the higher education setting, but these writings are remarkably sparse in number, leaving a tremendous need for future research and writing in this area. The writers within TQM, assessment, and benchmarking tend to use learning in very broad ways, with little explanation of what learning is, how it can occur, and the outcomes. Most of the literature is advocacy for learning rather than empirical data about how learning does occur. These writings and references are a poor place for higher education leaders to make judgments about whether to engage the concepts. Yet there has been change over time. A brief review of the literature demonstrates this shift and some promising trends for the use of organizational learning to higher education.

Coupling with Management Fads: TQM, Assessment, Benchmarking, and Accreditation

Most of the early references to the learning organization and the importance of learning were in the 1980s and early 1990s and were related to discussions of TQM or Continuous Quality Improvement (CQI) (Freed and Klugman, 1996; Freed, Klugman, and Fife, 1997). One of the main tenets of TQM and CQI is that for organizations to improve and remain competitive, the organizations and individuals within them must learn and evolve (Moore, 1996). TQM is a set of processes for helping to increase and encourage learning, such as human resource development, fear reduction, recognition and rewards, teamwork, and systematic problem solving (Birnbaum, 2000; Freed and Klugman, 1996). The aspects of TQM—teams, systems emphasis, mission, and learning—are strikingly similar to the learning organization. One of the main manifestations of this movement is the Malcolm Baldrige National Quality Awards that began in 1995 in which institutions using TQM processes compete to demonstrate their performance (Seymour and others, 1996).

However, some critics warn that learning within TQM is distinctive from organizational learning and the learning organization definitions; quality is conformance to requirements and about a highly controlled process (Birnbaum, 2000). The customer establishes requirements, and because quality is defined as customer satisfaction, learning is about a process of understanding customer needs and improving continually the processes that lead to customer satisfaction. Therefore, leaders thinking about using the term *learning* in conjunction with TQM have to realize that it tends to have a limited definition of learning. Furthermore, continuous learning tends to be more incremental in scope, focused on single-looped, not double-looped, learning. Many of the assumptions about learning are inconsistent with what we know about learning from organizational learning research. For example, TQM advocates the use of fact-based decision making; the organizational learning literature demonstrates that people are limited in being able to understand and combine multiple facts and perspectives related to complex decisions. In addition, the notion of "facts" existing is disputed in interpretive views of learning (Easterby-Smith, Araujo, and Burgoyne, 1999).

At the same time advocates were advancing TQM, policymakers were introducing assessment across the country as another way to improve the performance of higher education institutions (Banta, 1996; Freed, Klugman, and Fife, 1997; Lyons, 1999b). Assessment advocates also used the argument of organizational learning as a reason for engaging in assessment practices (in addition to accountability). It was commonsensical that higher education would be unable to improve its performance if it was unaware of how it was performing on a set of measures such as student learning. Assessment was a vehicle for promoting institutional learning to improve performance. The problem of narrowly defined learning also emerges within the assessment literature. There is an emphasis on learning that can be empirically measured and easily quantified. Yet problems that take place within organizations, as Senge (1990) points out, do not have simple causal relationships.

A related literature also refers to organizational learning, that is, benchmarking. Benchmarking is the process of studying other institutions for best practices and comparison to set goals for improving institutional performance (Alstete, 1995). Birnbaum (2000) uses the example of an admissions office staff that visits the admissions office of another institution that is considered more efficient and effective. It studies those processes and revises its own processes and goals based on this review, deciding to reduce its own cost by 10 percent in the next year. The benchmarking process is a technique for learning and is often referred to in the organizational learning literature as a way to obtain new ideas and foster experimentation (Garvin, 1993).

Yet within each of these fads—TQM and benchmarking—there is little reference to the concepts reviewed by the writers in the areas of organizational learning or the learning organization. Double-looped learning, inquiry and advocacy, and loosely coupled systems are not considered in the way learning is framed within these movements. The language and logic are closer to the application of the learning organization, with an emphasis on external threats to survival, advocacy of the wholesale good of learning, focus on techniques for learning without an understanding of how learning might occur in higher education, adoption of new techniques such as TQM or benchmarking rather than building on existing ones such as institutional research offices, and no attention to threats or limitations. Most likely, the coupling of learning with management fads such as TQM and benchmarking has resulted in some of the cynicism about organizational learning by professionals in higher education. The superficial references to learning breed skepticism among campus employees. The association of organizational learning with management fads has also led to overlooking the complexities of and threats to learning and in not investigating how learning occurs.

Current Uses of Organizational Learning: Beginning to Break Free of Management Fads

Although the literature on the learning organization in higher education continues to couple learning with TQM, benchmarking, and assessment, the use of organizational learning and the learning organization has been applied in new ways in the past decade. The logic behind the importance of organizational learning has evolved over the years in several ways: (1) a focus on principles from organizational learning, (2) concern with how learning actually occurs, (3) building on existing systems and processes as opposed to bringing in new approaches from business or with costly creation of new units, and (4) moving from external concerns for accountability and performance to more internal, ongoing processes of learning.

As Knowledge Management. Recently, the concept of organizational learning has been used to refer to the importance of creating knowledge management processes on campus (Edmonds and Spector, 2002). Knowledge management (KM) refers to the process in which organizations assess the data and information that exist within them, the processes in place to make the data and information meaningful and usable in the form of knowledge such as cross-institutional teams and effective use of data, and ways that knowledge and data can be maintained by the organization by attention to employee turnover and document management (Kidwell, Vander Linde, and Johnson, 2000; Marcum, 2001; Milam, 2001). KM emerged in response to the concern that it is not enough to have people learn within organizations; they also must be able to translate the learning into usable knowledge. Furthermore, the organization must be able to maintain knowledge within the organization as employees turn over or are promoted (Marcum, 2001; Milam, 2001). KM thus focuses more on how learning occurs rather than just on advocating a technique for learning, uses principles and concepts from organizational learning, and works within existing processes within colleges and universities, such as institutional research offices, to create learning.

Within higher education institutions, research offices, planning offices, and libraries are the target of much of this literature. Institutional research offices develop data for government reporting and campus decision making. However, data need to be translated into the appropriate format to be usable by campus stakeholders for decision making. There is a realization that on most campuses, people are unable to read the data produced and that both campus committees (asking for the appropriate data and in what format) and institutional research offices (understanding stakeholder needs better) need training in and attention to the development and use of data to translate the information into knowledge. Planning offices play a critical role in having expertise in data translation and use and in taking a systemic view of the organization. Libraries are also a main repository of campus data and resources for teaching and research, and in some cases for campus decision making. In addition, librarians are savvy with use of data and are important partners as campuses consider better ways to obtain data, create knowledge from data, and maintain knowledge within the organization (Kezar, 2003). Like planning offices, they often take a more systemwide view of campuses as they work cross-functionally with almost every unit on campus. Some writers within KM focus on the decision-making and problem-solving processes of leaders and managers in higher education, examining how learning actually occurs. One study examined Argyris and Schön's advocacy and inquiry model in order to explain leaders' problem solving (Tompkins, 2001). The results demonstrate that this approach to learning is underused by leaders in higher education and difficult to implement based on the multiple constituent groups on campus.

Lifelong Learning and Human Resource Management. As campuses begin to engage the notion of lifelong learning, they realize the need to rethink campus approaches to training and development (May, 1994). In the past, there has been limited discussion by administrators of colleges and universities about the importance of human resource management (Duke, 1999; May, 1994). Faculty, as professionals, were generally not considered candidates for development and training. Yet in the 1990s, faculty development offices emerged on almost every campus in the country. A growing literature base supports the effectiveness of faculty development and has begun to dispel this long-held myth that faculty do not need ongoing training; nevertheless, this myth remains pervasive on many campuses (Lieberman and Wehlburg, 2001). Many staff are deterred from taking advantage of staff development by supervisors who strictly define who can go and poor support for development (Martin, 1999; May, 1994). Yet studies also demonstrate the effectiveness of training sessions for employees' performance and learning. With a growing awareness of the importance of knowledge for effectiveness, this has implications for the importance of human resource offices and faculty development and other training groups on campuses that are often marginalized and have limited support in terms of funding and priority (May, 1994).

The role of human resource offices and faculty development is predicted to grow and play a more prominent role in the future (Bokeno and Gantt, 2000). A technique for creating lifelong learning among members of the campus and for encouraging learning is to implement a learning plan. The overall organization needs to have a plan in place for the learning needs across groups. Forest (2002) notes that most effective learning plans are aligned with the organization's strategic plan. The learning plan describes what a group of individuals hopes to learn in the process of achieving the goals described in the strategic plan. Forest provides a helpful example: "If a college's goal is to improve student retention, the members of that institution must seek to learn how various dimensions of the college affect current students and their retention, from the course registration process, to life in the residence halls, to perceived quality of teaching, to athletic facilities" (p. 33). Bringing learning into the strategic plan also brings human resource training and faculty development to the forefront of campus priorities. The literature from lifelong learning and human resource management emphasizes building on existing resources, systems, and structures to enable organizational learning; is embedded in assumptions from learning, not management theory; and focuses on barriers to learning, including hierarchy and professionalism (such as faculty status).

As Part of Collaborative and Socially Constructed Learning Pedagogy. Organizational learning is also being described in writing about collaborative or socially constructed forms of pedagogy (Boyce, 2003). More recent approaches to teaching stress the role of learning among all members on the campus, teachers and students, in creating knowledge (Ebbers and

Lenning, 1999), which breaks down the hierarchical relationships between learner and teacher. Some writers argue that campuses should use the metaphor of a learning community so that everyone on campus—faculty, administrators, staff, and students—sees their role as part of a process of organizational learning in the creation of a rich learning environment. Yet just as students are reluctant to give up their passive role as learners, employees are often unwilling or unable to see themselves as cofacilitators of learning. Researchers demonstrate that the traditional existence of hierarchical relationships among many groups on campus—, including faculty, administration, students, and academic affairs—the caste system relationship between faculty and support staff, and the patriarchal relationship between teacher and students prevents organizational learning from occurring within these environments (Flynn, 2000). Mental models based on hierarchical relationships dominate campuses. Also, divisions among groups make teamwork and collaboration difficult.

The learning organization itself reflects notions from socially constructed views of learning (Cullen, 1999). The emphasis on working in teams and of having groups work to develop a shared vision through sharing and discussion are important within a socially constructed view of knowledge where people work in groups toward the development of knowledge. Mental models are a recognition of one's own beliefs and views, but also a recognition that others may have differing beliefs that need to be understood and engaged toward the development of knowledge. Some faculty are suggesting that classrooms need to operate more as learning organizations that are based on concepts from social constructivism (Lyons, 1999a). This literature on collaborative learning focuses on barriers to learning and applies concepts from organizational learning such as mental models, teams, and problems of hierarchy. Also, organizational learning is being discussed in conjunction with the primary mission of the institution learning rather than being coupled with a management fad.

Insights from Exploration

The goal of this review of the literature on organizational learning and the learning organization within and outside higher education was to help leaders and change agents examine whether they might want to engage these approaches to organizational performance. Organizational learning and the learning organization were defined so that leaders can understand that one approach is more research based, but may offer less in terms of simple techniques or ideas for implementation, while the other is an idealized fad that can offer kernels of wisdom if used judiciously.

The review of the literature demonstrates that change agents and leaders need to be clear in referring to these concepts. It is likely that those on campus have heard these terms in conjunction with different approaches and management techniques and may be confused as to what they really mean. Distinguishing organizational learning from TQM, assessment, and benchmarking is needed for individuals to understand what is being proposed. Also, leaders need to be careful consumers of the existing literature base in higher education because it is unclear in defining learning, is generally not research based, and often is not critical of management techniques offered to encourage learning. Change agents should realize that people are skeptical of using organizational learning within campuses because employees will assume that they are referring to the learning organization fad, which is much more prevalent in the literature. They will have to work diligently to distinguish their efforts from the fad.

This examination of the literature also demonstrates that we know very little about how learning occurs in higher education. Only a handful of studies have empirically examined this issue. Almost all the literature in higher education is advocacy and anecdotally based. Until research is conducted, leaders need to turn to the business and nonprofit literature for advice about how to enable organizational learning (for example, Argyris and Schön, 1996; Garvin, 1993). However, research is needed within the higher education setting since this context is distinctive with tenure, long-term employees, a professional employee base, loosely coupled systems, and other distinctive elements that might affect how learning occurs. This review does highlight promising new directions in the literature: a move to use existing structures and units such as libraries, institutional research, and planning offices for enabling learning; and the beginnings of research on how learning occurs through examination of mistakes and use of cross-campus teams as well as barriers such as the hierarchical relations between groups.

Leaders may want to wait to initiate this approach until more research has been developed or at least to limit experimentation to areas where there has been some research, such as in knowledge management and cross-campus data teams. I say this with caution because trends in higher education, such as the continued diversification of the student body and staff, changes in technology, globalization, and marketization, suggest that higher education institutions need to learn, and learn quickly. Campuses may need to mine the organizational learning and learning organization concepts sooner rather than later for ways to meet daily challenges that require learning and change. I hope that the exploration in this chapter and the rest of the volume will help leaders become better informed to make this decision of whether and how to engage organizational learning and the learning organization.

References

Alpert, D., and Petrie, H. *What Is the Problem of Retrenchment in Higher Education?* 1982. (ED 217 771)

Alstete, J. *Benchmarking in Higher Education.* Washington, D.C.: George Washington University, 1995.

Argyris, C., and Schön, D. *Organizational Learning II.* Reading, Mass.: Addison-Wesley, 1996.

Banta, T. *Assessment in Practice*. San Francisco: Jossey Bass, 1996.

Birnbaum, R. *How Colleges Work*. San Francisco: Jossey-Bass, 1988.

Birnbaum, R. *Management Fads in Higher Education*. San Francisco: Jossey-Bass, 2000.

Bokeno, M., and Gantt, V. "Dialogic Mentoring: Core Relationships for Organizational Learning." *Management Communication Quarterly*, 2000, *14*, 237–270.

Boyce, M. "Organizational Learning Is Essential to Achieving and Sustaining Change in Higher Education." *Innovative Higher Education*, 2003, *28*(2), 119–137.

Cullen, J. "Socially Constructed Learning: A Commentary on the Concept of the Learning Organization." *Learning Organization*, 1999, *6*(1) 45–52.

Dierkes, M. *Handbook of Organizational Learning and Knowledge*. New York: Oxford University Press, 2001.

Duke, C. "Lifelong Learning: Implications for the University of the Twenty-First Century." *Higher Education Management*, 1999, *11*(1), 19–35.

Easterby-Smith, M., Araujo, L., and Burgoyne, J. (eds.). *Organizational Learning and the Learning Organization: Developments in Theory and Practice*. Thousand Oaks, Calif.: Sage, 1999.

Ebbers, L., and Lenning, O. *The Powerful Potential of Learning Communities: Improving Education of the Future*. Washington, D.C.: ASHE-ERIC, 1999.

Eckel, P., & Kezar, A. "Key Strategies For Making New Institutional Sense." *Higher Education Policy*, 2003, *16*(1), 39–53.

Edmonds, G., and Spector, M. *Knowledge Management in Institutional Design*. ERIC Digest, 2002. (ED 465 376)

Fiol, C., and Lyles, M. "Organizational Learning." *Academy of Management Review*, 1985, *71*(4), 81–91.

Flynn, W. "This Old House: Revitalizing Higher Education's Architecture." *Community College Journal*, 2000, *71*(1), 36–39.

Forest, J. "Learning Organizations: Higher Education Institutions Can Work Smarter Too." *Connection*, 2002, pp. 31–32.

Freed, J., and Klugman, M. "Higher Education Institutions as Learning Organizations: The Quality Principles and Practices in Higher Education." Paper presented at the Association for the Study of Higher Education Annual Meeting, June 1996, in Richmond, Virginia. (ED 402 845)

Freed, J., Klugman, M., and Fife, J. *A Culture of Academic Excellence*. Washington, D.C.: George Washington University, 1997.

Garvin, D. "Building a Learning Organization." *Harvard Business Review*, 1993, *71*(4), 78–91.

Huber, G. "Organizational Learning: The Contributing Processes and the Literature." *Organization Science*, 1991, *2*(2), 88–115.

Jeris, L. "Intervening for Transformation: An Organizational Learning Perspective." 1998. (ED 420 295)

Kezar, A. *The Role of Integrator: Potential Opportunities for Librarians to Connect NSSE to Institutional Improvement*. Washington, D.C.: American Association for Higher Education, 2003.

Kidwell, J., Vander Linde, K., and Johnson, S. "Applying Corporate Knowledge Management Practices in Higher Education." *EDUCAUSE Quarterly*, 2000, *4*, 28–33.

Levitt, B., and March, J. "Organizational Learning." *Annual Review of Sociology*, 1988, *14*, 319–340.

Lieberman, D., and Wehlburg, C. (eds.). "To Improve the Academy: Resources for Faculty, Instructional, and Organizational Development." *Portland State University Report*, 2001, *19*.

Lyons, P. *Classroom as Learning Organization: Changing Assumptions and Processes*. 1999a. (ED 384 304)

Lyons, P. *Assessment Techniques to Enhance Organizational Learning*. 1999b. (ED 426 678)

Marcum, J. "From Information Center to Discovery System: Next Step for Librarians?" *Journal of Academic Librarianship,* 2001, 27(2), 97–106.

Martin, E. *Changing Academic Work: Developing the Learning University.* London, England: Society for Research into Higher Education, 1999.

May, S. "Beyond 'Super Secretary' Courses: Revisioning Staff Development in Learning Organizations." *Canadian Journal of University Continuing Education,* 1994, 20(2), 45–54.

Milam, J. "Knowledge Management for Higher Education." *ERIC Digest,* 2001. (ED 464 520)

Moore, N. *Using the Malcolm Baldrige Criteria to Improve Quality in Higher Education.* 1996. (ED 399 919)

Neumann, A. *Making Mistakes: Error and Learning in the College Presidency.* 1988. (ED 298 810)

Schein, E. *Organizational Culture and Leadership.* San Francisco: Jossey Bass, 1985.

Senge, P. *The Fifth Discipline.* New York: Doubleday, 1990.

Seymour, D., and others. *High Performing Colleges: The Malcolm Baldrige National Quality Award as a Framework for Improving Higher Education.* 1996. (ED 393 342)

Tompkins, T. "Using Advocacy and Inquiry to Improve the Thinking Process of Future Managers." *Journal of Management Education,* 2001, 25(5), 553–571.

ADRIANNA KEZAR is associate professor at the University of Southern California in the Higher Education Administration Program.

2

This chapter describes a project in which teams of faculty, administrators, and staff from fourteen colleges and universities engaged in organizational learning for the purposes of identifying and improving inequitable educational outcomes for African American and Latino students.

Promoting Organizational Learning in Higher Education to Achieve Equity in Educational Outcomes

Georgia L. Bauman

Colleges and universities have been highlighted as an example of a type of organization that does not engage in organizational learning effectively (Dill, 1999; Garvin, 1993). While learning is the central work of these institutions, they are believed to lack the attributes needed for organizational learning. According to David Garvin (1993), for an entity to be a learning organization, it must acquire new ideas that lead to improvements in the way it does business. Garvin contends that "many universities fail to qualify [because] . . . these organizations have been effective at creating or acquiring new knowledge but notably less successful in applying that knowledge to their own activities" (p. 80). For example, colleges and universities have made considerable investments in technology and training to develop their capacity to collect all kinds of information about students, ranging from their incoming SAT scores through every course they take to their graduating grade point averages (GPAs). In addition, higher education now finds itself in an "age of accountability" (Alexander, 2000; Gumport and Sporn, 1999; Ohmann, 1999; Radner, 1996; Sewall, 1996) in which institutions are required to provide innumerable data to outside agencies. Despite this, very little organizational learning is culled from these data. The Knight Higher Educational Collaborative (2000) asserts, "Today, universities and colleges expend more time, effort, and money than ever before in gathering data. . . . For all that, higher education institutions still have not learned to organize and use data effectively for internal decisions or public accountability" (p. 5).

I engaged in a qualitative study of the Diversity Scorecard project for which the primary goal was to promote organizational learning among faculty, staff, and administrators about inequities in educational outcomes for African American and Latino students on their campuses. The project posited the problem of inequitable educational outcomes for African American and Latino students in higher education as a problem in institutional performance—one that might be remedied through organizational learning. Often, low achievement among minority students as reflected in retention and graduation rates is attributed to their precollege characteristics, preparation, attitudes, and behaviors that are indicative of their commitment to educational goals, their perceptions of family expectations, their academic and social integration, and the academic and cultural capital they possess. (See, for example, Braxton, 2000; Kraemer, 1997; Jun and Tierney, 1999; Rendón and Valadez, 1993; Tinto, 1993.) In this approach, the responsibility for learning is placed primarily on the student. This project took a different approach. Rather than focusing on the deficits that prevent African American and Latino students from succeeding in higher education, the project proposed that institutional actors (faculty, staff, administrators) become responsible for the learning needed to improve educational outcomes for these students.

In the Diversity Scorecard project, teams of faculty, staff, and administrators at fourteen colleges and universities engaged in the examination of evidence—factual, existing institutional data—that revealed actual conditions about the state of equity in educational outcomes for African Americans and Latinos. The teams sought to answer questions such as, "Do African American and Latino students graduate in all majors equitably or are they concentrated in particular fields? Do they graduate with GPAs as high as students in other groups, rendering them competitive for admission to graduate school? Are African American and Latino students overrepresented among students who require remedial coursework and underrepresented among those who are members of the honors program and other elite academic programs?" by examining institutional data as a group.

Stemming from the notion that organizational learning can play an important role in improving institutional performance, the premise of this project was that the examination of institutional data disaggregated by race and ethnicity can be an effective means of revealing inequities in educational outcomes. My interest focused on whether the analysis of such data could prompt college and university actors to recognize the inequities in educational outcomes on their campuses. Could the consideration of simple but specific indicators of educational outcomes, such as choice of majors, GPA, and completion of remedial and developmental courses, raise awareness about the stratification of achievement along ethnic and racial lines?

I sought to answer these questions by observing and documenting the learning, which I define as being the development of new recognition of the problem, that took place in the fourteen teams at fourteen higher education institutions in southern California. Although the organizational learning literature is rich in concepts about how learning happens and what serves as evidence of an organization's having learned, there is a dearth of empirical studies of how organizational learning happens. For the most part, organizational learning theory is not based on observations of behavior within organizations, and its conceptions are exceedingly broad, encompassing nearly all aspects of organizational change. Thus, the method used in this research overcame two problems in the study of organizational learning: (1) the lack of empirical documentation of how learning happens in a group and (2) the tendency to discuss organizational learning at an abstract level rather than in relation to a particular problem. I observed in real time the learning that took place in the team meetings and documented it in field notes as it was happening.

I found that organizational learning was promoted among the groups when three conditions existed: the presence of new ideas, the cultivation of doubt in existing knowledge and practices, and the development and transfer of knowledge among institutional actors. These three conditions are consistent with the organizational learning literature. Five of the fourteen groups were found to be high learning groups, which means they reflected the practices described in the organizational learning literature such as examining mental models. Data provided the key to promoting group learning by (1) generating new ideas among team members and (2) prompting team members to question common knowledge about educational outcomes at their institution. The interaction as teams were examining the data was also important for what I came to call group learning. There was a clear contrast between teams that examined institutional data as a group and those that relied on one person's knowledge rather than exploring the data together.

Presence of New Ideas

Acquiring new knowledge and ideas is the first step toward learning (Garvin, 1993; Huber, 1991). Although new ideas are essential for learning, they do not guarantee that learning will follow. New ideas can be acquired from one's own experience, the experiences and best practices of other individuals or organizations, and experimentation (Garvin, 1993; Huber, 1991; Levitt and March, 1988).

Examining existing institutional data in novel ways and asking new questions about routine data can also provide new ideas and information. Garvin (1993) believes that colleges and universities do not apply the research skills used for other purposes to institutional self-study and improvement. We feel this is true to the extent that institutional actors do not typically ask questions about institutional data comparable to those they might ask for research projects in other areas. The Knight Higher Education Collaborative (2000), which is composed of educational leaders and researchers, asserts that institutional data can provide the answers to questions such as these: "Who starts but does not finish, and why? What is being learned, and for what purpose?" (p. 8). Delving into institutional data has the potential to provide new ideas and knowledge about institutional effectiveness and performance.

When teams examined data as a group, new ideas occurred to them. Some team members had examined many of these data individually before they became involved in the Diversity Scorecard project. However, they had not looked at them disaggregated by ethnic and racial categories. Like a bifocal lens, these categories provided fresh perspectives on old data. This was evidenced in two ways. First, increased awareness of inequities in student outcomes prompted many team members to ask new questions about their causes and consequences. Second, the high learning groups tended to mine the data more deeply and engage in a second-order level of inquiry.

The high learning groups learned a great deal more about the inequities in educational outcomes for African American and Latino students on their campuses. For example, when studying data related to retention, one team discovered that white and Asian American students tended to leave the institution in good academic standing, while African American and Latino students tended to do so while on academic probation:

> The rates were disaggregated into 4 . . . categories: (1) those who persisted in good standing, (2) those who persisted but were on academic probation, (3) those who did not persist who were in good standing, and (4) those who did not persist who had been on probation. What [the participant] was surprised by and pointed out was that there was a significant number who left who were in good standing, even among transfer students, and they tended to be White or Asian American.

Another team made a similar finding:

> [The member] said he learned many things from the data, but one thing that stood out was what he learned about students who had transferred to this institution from a community college. He said he never realized how many transfer students leave after one year and how that differs widely by ethnicity.

Before examining the data disaggregated by race and ethnicity, many team members had a somewhat simplified notion of who left the institution and who was retained; moreover, they were unaware of marked differences according to race and ethnicity.

Over the course of the first year of the project, several participants commented that this approach to data examination was new to them and had led them to new discoveries. For example, a participant commented that he had "never thought about gateway courses—ever." (A gateway course acts as a prerequisite for particular majors or programs or a generally required course for graduation, and a student's success or failure in such a course might limit his or her options or the ability to graduate. For example, calculus is a prerequisite for engineering. A student who does not pass calculus cannot declare engineering as his or her major.) Another participant compared the method to her previous experiences: "This is the first time that I'm aware of that anyone is looking at this problem by ethnicity and to this level of detail. [People at our institution] tend to use global, crude measures. With this project we can look at the subtleties of the data."

Another participant observed, "We have a chance to look at where we are. We can make arguments supported with the numbers. Maybe we could even ask some new questions."

To create new ideas from existing institutional data on one's own campus as the Diversity Scorecard teams did, one might consider examining data that are traditionally reported externally, such as to accrediting bodies and to fulfill state and federal reporting requirements, in novel ways. Examine these data by racial/ethnic categories, gender, those who receive Pell grants versus those who do not, and other characteristics that may reveal differences in achievement and educational outcomes. Ask new questions of the data. For example, on an annual basis, the institution's graduation rates are reported. A new question that may generate new ideas would be, "What are the GPAs of our graduating class disaggregated by race and ethnicity? Do African American students graduate with GPAs comparable to other groups?"

Promoting Doubt in Existing Knowledge and Practices

Weick (1979) developed a model of how groups (or organizations) reduce the multiple meanings their members hold about a phenomenon to a shared, common understanding that can serve as the basis for group action in the future. He did not call this learning; he called it the "organizing" process. Weick theorized that something in the environment triggers this process, which is dependent on communication and interaction among group members. When some event or piece of information catches the group's attention, its members engage in cycles of communication, restricted by rules and norms embedded in the culture of the group or the organization within which they operate. Eventually they reach some sort of common understanding, which is then stored in some manner for future use. For example, the faculty of a particular college may believe that they serve all members of their diverse student population equitably. That common understanding has been "stored" in the culture of the college.

Like other organizational theorists (Argyris and Schön, 1978; March, 1991), Weick (1979) suggests that organizations learn when these stored understandings and information are called into question. When organizational actors doubt what they have traditionally believed to be true, an opportunity for learning arises. Organizations should treat the "past as a pest" (p. 221) and question such retained information as routines, norms, rules, and other elements of the organization's culture and operations, which are often considered sacrosanct and immutable. Unfortunately, "the thick layering of routines in most organizations, coupled with the fact that departures from routine increase vulnerability, mean that discrediting is rare" (p. 225).

Textual analysis indicated that members of the high learning groups were more open than those of other teams in terms of questioning and challenging common knowledge about their institution, its students, and the practices they engaged in. This resulted from their giving priority to what the data revealed rather than to other sources of information, such as experience-based or anecdotal knowledge. Teams that were not in the high learning category tended to use other sources of information to rationalize what the data revealed. For example, in one case, the data showed that Latino students transferred to four-year institutions at lower rates than white students did, and when they did transfer, they tended to go to the lower-tier state university nearby rather than the more elite institution farther away. This was the explanation given:

> In our discussion of access to four-year institutions, [the participant] stated that there might be a number of reasons that more of their students transfer to [the local public institution] rather than [to the more elite university system]. [The participant] explained that location might be one of them. Possibly because the [lower-tier institution] is closer to [their geographical area] than [the more elite institution], students might want to transfer to some place closer to home.
>
> [Another team member] explained that this may be a bigger issue for Latino students because of pressure from family to remain close to home.

When the low numbers of Latino students transferring to the more elite university were attributed to family pressure, the statement went unchallenged by other members of the team. By allowing supposition to take precedence over what the data might indicate, the team lost an opportunity to learn from the data or to question their own knowledge and practices.

In contrast, the high learning groups treated their own knowledge as hypotheses to be proved or disproved by the data. One participant commented, "This project is training me to think critically. I now look at some of the mythologies and ask about supportive data." As the teams examined data, commonly held assumptions or myths were challenged, and in some instances their understandings of the "way things are" were disproved:

> In brainstorming goals [participant A] said that overall the university has a high retention rate for Latinas but a dismal retention rate for African-American women. "African-American women are the most at-risk at [our institution]. I want to know why there is this unexpected difference."
>
> [The institutional research member] disagreed, referring to the data, "Actually African-American males are doing worse." [Participant A] was surprised and remarked, "Then I've been hearing incorrect information."

Doubts were also raised about particular areas within the college or university, as well as the institution's overall performance in serving African American and Latino students. When one team examined data showing that students who pass the remedial course sequence do not go on to succeed in the college-level courses, a participant questioned the curriculum on which the remedial sequence is based:

> [The participant] went on to say that a large percent of part time faculty teach the remedial courses. They all use the same workbook and common curriculum approach. "Why do they not prepare the students for the transition to college level courses?" She said maybe the "cookbook" they're using is not the right one.

After another team discussed data reflecting student outcomes, a participant expressed doubt about the value that attending the institution adds to the students while they are at the institution and whether they prepare the students for postgraduate life.

> Yes, we are very diverse, but what does that mean to us as an institution? I want to be able to say, "Yes, we have these diverse students and we're the best at what we do [educating and graduating students]." But, I wonder what value do we add to the students while they are here? What are they prepared to do when they leave?

The high learning groups were prepared to doubt and question their own knowledge and practices and accept what the data revealed, even if that disproved the assumptions under which they had been operating. This approach to the data promoted group learning.

Although it is difficult to pinpoint what led to some teams' willingness to question and doubt what they thought to be true, there seemed to be a team orientation that facilitated the cultivation of such doubt. These teams did not view their engagement in the project as a task to be finished and crossed off their collective to-do list. They approached the project as a process or a journey with no clear end. Their primary goal was to learn about the inequities in educational outcomes that existed on their campuses; it was not to complete the Diversity Scorecard and the report to the president. This learning orientation may have made it easier to give each other the time and space to reflect on what the data revealed; there was no rush to find an answer, and it was acceptable, if not desirable, to continually bring up challenging and uncomfortable questions. In the groups in which doubt was not cultivated, it was more problematic and more likely to be perceived as negative when someone brought up a question or concern that may add complexity to the problem under study as well as work load to the team.

To cultivate doubt on one's own campus is a difficult task. Perhaps the easiest way to accomplish this is to bring in an outsider, as was done in this project. The outsider should be unfamiliar with and unattached to the campus culture and norms. An outsider can act in a manner different from those situated inside the culture and ask the seemingly ignorant questions as well as those questions that may not be safe for an insider to ask without negative consequences. When bringing in an outside consultant is not possible, we must force ourselves to take an outsider's view of our own institutions in order to question the norms and beliefs that are part of the institutional fabric. One method to accomplish this is to create teams of individuals who have very disparate roles on campus—people from academic affairs, student affairs, faculty from varied disciplines, students, and others—such that on any given topic, someone in the group could function as the outsider. Bensimon and Neumann (1993) discuss "real" versus "illusory" teams, and one of the most important distinctions of real teams is that they fulfill a cognitive function which "enlarges the intelligence span of individual team members" (p. 41); in other words, many heads are better than one. This intelligence span is expanded by valuing the multiple perspectives that individual team members may have on a given issue or problem. Bensimon and Neumann write, "Reconsidering a problem through multiple lenses might make the problem look more complex and might make a person feel that the problem is becoming less and less manageable. However, as a problem unfolds in its largeness . . . previously hidden facets may suggest solutions not seen when it was defined in simpler terms" (p. 42).

Also, over time, the campus leadership and community at large could try to make the practice of cultivating doubt and questioning the campus mythologies and asking for evidence part of the institutional culture. These practices could become accepted and respected in departments, on committees, and among other working groups.

Development and Transfer of Knowledge Among Institutional Actors

Information, or data, and knowledge play important roles in organizational learning. According to Daft and Huber (1987), organizational learning occurs along two dimensions: the systems-structural dimension, which focuses on the acquisition and distribution of information, and the interpretive dimension, which involves the interpretation of that information. Interpretation and understanding of information by institutional actors are associated with knowledge. Daft and Huber observe that "organizations undertake both types of activity" (p. 10) and that both activities contribute to organizational learning.

Davenport and Prusak (1998) define data as "a set of discrete, objective facts about events" (p. 2). Kock (1999) refers to data as "carriers" of information and knowledge. Brown and Duguid (2000) regard data and information as being distinct and different from knowledge because they are independent of people, existing in a self-contained state in documents or databases. Consequently, having documents or databases does not imply understanding or knowledge; they are repositories of unprocessed facts, available for interpretation.

Knowledge is "broader, deeper, and richer than data or information" (Davenport and Prusak, 1998, p. 5). Contained within the mind, it results from an amalgamation of experiences, personal values, personal characteristics, and interactions with others. We use knowledge to interpret, evaluate, and incorporate new experiences and interactions. Because it is dependent on knowers, the exchange and creation of knowledge take place within and between humans. The field of knowledge management is concerned with managing, transferring, and maximizing the knowledge held in organizational actors' minds for improvement of the organization as a whole. To find out what actors know, organizations set up structures to promote social interaction for the purposes of sharing and creating knowledge. Those who study organizations consider this transfer of knowledge to be an essential ingredient of organizational learning (Daft and Huber, 1987; Garvin, 1993; Huber, 1991; Levitt and March, 1988).

A structure that promotes the creation and transfer of knowledge among organizational members is commonly called a group. Alternatively, such a body may be referred to as a team, committee, task force, or council. Cutscher-Gershenfeld and others (1998) define team-based work systems as "complex amalgams of tangible practices and intangible elements such as interpersonal interactions" that promote "the creation of knowledge within the firm" (p. 59). This emphasis on teams and teamwork in business has been described as "parallel to the emphasis on cooperative learning in schools, colleges, and continuing education . . . through which students work together to maximize their own and each other's learning" (Sormunen-Jones, Chalupa, and Charles, 2000, p. 154). To a great extent, higher education operates through small working groups called committees that are responsible for making the most critical decisions within their respective institutions. Every college or university has its curriculum committees within departments, promotion and tenure committees, planning and enrollment management committees, and any number of ad hoc committees. It seems logical to assume that these committees are the working groups most likely to benefit from their institutions' numerous stores of information. In view of the abundance of available data, two key questions come to mind: Can committees turn these data into knowledge? If so, will this knowledge provide the committee members with a different or better understanding of the issues they must address? This framework was tested by observing and recording the group learning—the development of new recognitions of inequity in educational outcomes—of the committees involved in this project.

The high learning groups spent the majority of their meeting time throughout the year examining data as a team. Usually the institutional research member would bring copies of several data tables for everyone. He or she would explain what the data represented; then there would be several minutes for the team members to review the data for themselves. This was followed by two hours of discussion about what the data revealed, what the areas of inequity were, what this might mean for the institution, and other topics. In teams that were not considered high learning groups, one of two scenarios occurred. In some instances, the team would use the data only to confirm what they already believed to be true. They would consult data to make sure that this information backed up their claims. In other cases, the team would ask the institutional research member to review the data outside the meetings and provide them with a report. Because there was no ongoing discussion, exchange of questions, or brainstorming, this approach limited what could be learned from the data.

Data often confirmed what members of the high learning groups suspected: that greater numbers of African American students fail mathematics courses, for example. However, by examining and discussing the data, it seemed that the information was transformed into knowledge. This is demonstrated in the following observation recorded in the field notes.

> While none of the data really seemed to surprise anyone present, the team members seemed to really process the ideas and problems that the data revealed and internalized this "proof" of what they already knew/suspected to be the case. What may have been "hunches" or assumptions became knowledge based upon data. . . . The data/information also generated a lot of discussion among the group, such that the data served as a foundation or building block for more knowledge and ideas. For example, in looking at the gateway courses, the observer asked whether there were math prerequisites for economics. They all discovered/learned that there are no prerequisites for economics, although perhaps there should be given the high failure rates in the course.

I considered the high learning groups to be "communities of practice" (Wenger, 1998) that are participating in situated learning (Lave and Wenger, 1991). Communities of practice are typically small groups within larger organizations that are drawn together by "expertise and passion" (Wenger and Snyder, 2000, p. 139) in a particular area and meet on a regular basis over an extended period of time. For the purposes of this project, a particularly valuable form of learning came from having a team within an institution engage in an inquiry about the state of equity on their own campus (Lave and Wenger, 1991). If this project conformed to the typical academic research model, the research team would have presented groups at the participating institutions with findings about equity based on the results of surveys, interviews, or analyses of demographic trends. Such an approach would have been more efficient, faster, and less costly, but the results would soon have been forgotten. In the context of this project, situated learning means that faculty and staff from the participating institutions are themselves engaged in the inquiry; they are not the subjects of someone else's study or passive recipients of the findings of others (Lave and Wenger, 1991). A community of practice provides the situation and establishes the conditions for effective learning, which can bring about important changes in the beliefs, values, and actions of individuals.

The opportunity for institutional change lies in the possibility that individual participants will transfer their learning to other contexts within the institution and thereby enable others to learn and to change. Several team members spoke of trying to apply what they had learned to their work at the institution—for example:

> I'm trying to work out ways I can apply the knowledge I've gained here [in our team] more this semester. I share what I've learned with the Dean of Student Life. . . . I have used some of the statistics in conversations. I just had a conversation with some faculty and the BSU [Black Student Union]. I want to use some of the data in conversations with student leaders. This is not a broad-based dissemination yet, but it's useful.

Teams that did not examine and discuss the data as a group were quite limited in terms of what they could learn. They continued to rely on what others reported to them, and this was not transformed into knowledge.

Higher education institutions already have many established committees, often formed around problems (for example, in response to a campus crisis) or decisions or changes that need to be made (for example, hiring committees and restructuring committees). However, it is rare that such committees take a learning approach to their task. They do not take time to research, define, and understand the problem before trying to find the solution. Taking a learning rather than a task orientation to the problem, decision, or change that defines their charge, the group could create the time and space for discussion and learning from one another in order to create knowledge on which they can act. In the Diversity Scorecard project, the teams were essentially presidentially appointed, although in most cases, the president delegated the task of forming the team to one person. One might expect that those teams whose members were most committed to equity or the use of data to promote organizational learning would be the most effective communities of practice. This was not the case. Each of the high learning groups had individual members who were initially quite skeptical of the project, its aims, and its methods. What made these groups effective in terms of learning about inequities in educational outcomes was that they consistently acted in a manner that supported a learning approach to the problem.

Conclusion

While disagreeing with Garvin's view (1993) that higher education institutions do not engage in learning, I agree with his observation that colleges and universities do not learn as effectively as they could. Institutional actors are capable of applying their practices as communities of researchers to studies of the institution itself. Therefore, faculty who conduct research in economics, sociology, business, the study of organizations, and many other fields can use their research methods for the assessment and improvement of their own institutions. Teams composed of such researchers ought to examine data that are relevant to the charge just as they would examine data for a funded research project. The study and improvement of our own institutions should be as rigorous as our study of other types of institutions and social structures.

Ewell (1997) concurs that data are critical to institutional learning and improvement, and he suggests that becoming what is referred to in the literature as a learning organization "involves creating institutional capacities for gathering and interpreting data at all levels" (p. 6). This implies that an organization should not only gather and store data but also engage in its analysis. Institutional research should involve more than administrative and reporting functions. At the lower levels of the organization, "concrete mechanisms for gathering data, and the incentives to use them are equally important" (p. 6).

These suggestions indicate other ways in which postsecondary institutions can increase their capacity for ongoing learning and self-study for the purposes of institutional improvement. The potential for institutional learning exists, but institutional improvement depends on the effectiveness of faculty and staff in putting this learning into action. Accountability reports and other routine reporting mechanisms may provide an excellent starting point for the exploration of problems in institutional performance. O'Neil, Bensimon, Diamond, and Moore (1999) found that when they approached an accountability initiative as an opportunity for institutional self-assessment and improvement, it had "latent benefits that contribute to organizational well-being" (p. 40). Even an accountability report can generate new ideas and call common knowledge into question, and when a group can come together to study and discuss what is revealed by such a report, information can be transformed into knowledge. In this study, the high learning groups experienced the highest levels of group learning about inequities in educational outcomes among students of different ethnic groups because of their attention to and thorough examination of data.

References

Alexander, K. "The Changing Face of Accountability." *Journal of Higher Education*, 2000, 71(4), 411–431.

Argyris, C., and Schön, D. A. "Organizational Learning." In D. S. Pugh (ed.), *Organization Theory*. New York: Penguin Books, 1978.

Bensimon, E. M., and Neumann, A. *Redesigning Collegiate Leadership: Teams and Team Work in Higher Education*. Baltimore, Md.: Johns Hopkins University Press, 1993.

Braxton, J. M. *Reworking the Student Departure Puzzle*. Nashville, Tenn.: Vanderbilt University Press, 2000.

Brown, J. S., and Duguid, P. *The Social Life of Information*. Boston: Harvard Business School Press, 2000.

Cutscher-Gershenfeld, J., and others. *Knowledge-Driven Work: Unexpected Lessons from Japanese and United States Work Practices*. New York: Oxford University Press, 1998.

Daft, R. L., and Huber, G. P. "How Organizations Learn: A Communication Framework." *Research in the Sociology of Organizations*, 1987, *5*, 1–36.

Davenport, T. H., and Prusak, L. *Working Knowledge: How Organizations Manage What They Know.* Boston: Harvard Business School Press, 1998.

Dill, D. D. "Academic Accountability and University Adaptation: The Architecture of an Academic Learning Organization." *Higher Education*, 1999, *38*, 127–154.

Ewell, P. T. "Organizing for Learning: A New Imperative." *AAHE Bulletin*, Dec. 1997, pp. 3–6.

Garvin, D. A. "Building a Learning Organization." *Harvard Business Review*, 1993, *71*(4), 78–91.

Gumport, P. J., and Sporn, B. "Institutional Adaptation: Demands for Management Reform and University Administration." In J. C. Smart and W. G. Tierney (eds.), *Higher Education: Handbook of Theory and Research.* New York: Agathon Press, 1999.

Huber, G. P. "Organizational Learning: The Contributing Processes and the Literatures." *Organization Science*, 1991, *2*(1), 88–115.

Jun, A., and Tierney, W. G. "At-Risk Urban Students and College Success: A Framework for Effective Preparation." *Metropolitan Universities*, 1999, *9*(4), 49–59.

Knight Higher Education Collaborative. "The Data Made Me Do It." *Policy Perspectives*, 2000, *9*(2), 1–12.

Kock, N. *Process Improvement and Organizational Learning: The Role of Collaboration Technologies.* Hershey, Pa.: Idea Group Publishing, 1999.

Kraemer, B. A. "The Academic and Social Integration of Hispanic Students into College." *Review of Higher Education*, 1997, *20*(2), 163–179.

Lave, J., and Wenger, E. *Situated Learning: Legitimate Peripheral Participation.* Cambridge, England: Cambridge University Press, 1991.

Levitt, B., and March, J. G. "Organizational Learning." *Annual Review of Sociology*, 1988, *14*, 319–340.

March, J. G. "Exploration and Exploitation in Organizational Learning." *Organization Science*, 1991, *2*(1), 71–87.

Ohmann, R. M. "Historical Reflections on Accountability." *Radical Teacher*, 1999, *57*, 2–7.

O'Neil, H. F., Bensimon, E. M., Diamond, M. A., and Moore, K. "Designing and Implementing an Academic Scorecard." *Change*, 1999, *31*(6), 32–40.

Radner, S. G. "Accountability, Evaluation of Tenured Faculty, and Program Reviews." *Radical Teacher*, 1996, *48*, 11–12.

Rendón, L. I., and Valadez, J. R. "Qualitative Indicators of Hispanic Student Transfer." *Community College Review*, 1993, *20*(4), 27–37.

Sewall, A. "From the Importance of Education in the '80s to Accountability in the '90s." *Education*, 1996, *116*(3), 325–332.

Sormunen-Jones, C., Chalupa, M. R., and Charles, T. A. "The Dynamics of Gender Impact on Group Achievement." *Delta Pi Epsilon Journal*, 2000, *42*(3), 154–170.

Tinto, V. *Leaving College.* (2nd ed.) Chicago: University of Chicago Press, 1993.

Weick, K. E. *The Social Psychology of Organizing.* (2nd ed.) New York: McGraw-Hill, 1979.

Wenger, E. *Communities of Practice: Learning, Meaning and Identity.* Cambridge, England: Cambridge University Press, 1998.

Wenger, E., and Snyder, W. M. "Communities of Practice: An Organizational Frontier." *Harvard Business Review*, 2000, *78*(1), 139–145.

GEORGIA L. BAUMAN is the director for instructional services at Santa Monica College in Los Angeles, California.

3

This chapter uses the conceptual framework of a learning organization to make a case for how a theory might enrich organizational practice in the field of higher education.

Community Service as Learning

Jodi L. Anderson

What better candidate than an institution of higher education, you might ask, for the adoption of a learning organization framework? While the concept of a learning organization would seem to be logically applied to institutions of higher education, given that they themselves are entities designed to retain, produce, and disseminate knowledge, this framework is much more commonly applied in business and management fields. In fact, it is only in the past few decades that the idea of a learning organization has become more widely embraced by theorists (Argyris and Schön, 1996). The concept of organizations as learning systems can be traced back to the decision-making approach model by Simon and March and the work of Argyris (1982) on double-loop learning. While many in the 1970s had difficulty accepting the idea that organizations could learn (such processes were associated only with individual human learning), constructing an image of organizations as more monolithic and impersonal entities (often more easily identified by those external to the organization) helped give the concept firmer grounding and acceptance (Argyris and Schön, 1996).

As Kezar points out in Chapter Four, these early views of learning organizations were rooted in the cognitive theories of the day, and for that reason they reflected a more narrowly defined conception of learning. Morgan (1997) describes the key principles of such organizations, which he terms "cybernetic," as having the capacity to perceive, monitor, and scan relevant aspects of their environment; the ability to relate received information back to those guiding the system; the ability to detect significant ruptures or problems; and the ability to initiate actions when necessary for system stability. Other variations of the learning organization include viewing organizations as brains or cybernetic systems (Morgan, 1997) and as self-regulating machines (Birnbaum, 1988). Consistent with Kezar's critique of learning organizations as demonstrating an overreliance on more narrowly defined, mechanistic views of learning, Senge (1990) affirms the value of multiple intelligences that have historically not been valued. As such, he moves our conception of the learning organization toward a more authentic view of how individuals' intuition and personal fulfillment affect organizational processes and can further organizational learning. It is this more expansive notion of learning that is used throughout this chapter.

Why a Learning Organization Framework for the Engaged Institution?

In the past few decades, critiques centering on how public universities must better serve societal needs have spurred creative thinking about the need for institutional change. Tierney (1998) writes of the need for universities to be "more responsive" to their customers; Boyer (1990) suggests a reconceptualization of faculty roles through the adoption of a framework of teaching, integration, application, and discovery; Walshok (1995) expands the vision of how universities contribute to economic vitality and community wellness; and Boyte and Hollander (1999) challenge institutions to exercise more intentionality in educating students for their civic responsibilities. One clear institutional response to these calls for increased engagement is a focus on strengthening external networks by partnering with communities. In this chapter, the adoption of the learning organization framework is put forth as a foundation that has the potential to broadly affect institutional practice and, in doing so, foster partnership work that is responsive to societal needs. Applying concepts from this organizational lens can strengthen innovative responsiveness to existing critiques of higher education.

In this chapter, university and community partnerships are defined as relationships formed between the university and community to create a reciprocal flow of resources that broadly benefit the campus and surrounding communities. It is important to note that universities can establish partnerships with external constituencies in a number of ways, but it is the development of partnerships between campus and nonprofit community-based entities to address social needs that is the focus here.

A variety of perspectives have been brought to bear on the study of university and community partnerships. First is a focus on exploring how partnerships may be necessary for institutional self-preservation. These efforts illuminate how institutions seek to combat charges that they engage in work disconnected from real societal issues and that institutions are primarily self-serving rather than society serving. In short, this perspective seeks to address societal critiques of the ivory tower and explore how universities might better balance a desire for autonomy with a stronger commitment to public accountability. Second is a body of literature that approaches the study of university and community partnerships from a pragmatic or functionalist perspective, the idea being that partnerships are of unique value because they address certain external social problems more effectively or more efficiently than either individual entity would if functioning alone (LeGates and Robinson, 1998). And third, a number of case studies of university and community partnerships provide evidence of the cultural and logistical challenges inherent in establishing and sustaining individual partnerships (Braskamp and Wergin, 1999; Weiwel and Lieber, 1998; Maurrasse, 2001). This chapter provides a less common, yet critical, perspective: how universities through the adoption of a learning organization framework might better understand the benefits that accrue to their institutions—namely, maximizing organizational capacity—through an increased focus on community engagement. This unique perspective informs existing work by provoking thinking about how partnerships are not just necessary for institutional survival but can enhance institutional functioning generally. By looking at partnerships as not just a marginal effort but as indicative of a fundamental shift in thinking about how an organization can maximize its own functioning, movement toward the engaged institution is more genuinely institutionalized. Therefore, institutional preservation is seen not as the driving goal but rather as a natural outgrowth of a fundamental shift in institutional processes undergirded by a learning framework.

Organizational Realities in Public Research Universities

One of the reasons that universities are so well suited for the adoption of organizational learning principles is their unique structure. Due to their complexity, they are often referred to as "organized anarchies" (Cohen and March, 1974). They are large, differentiated organizations with many functioning units that work in an independent fashion. As Kerr (2001) noted in his study of the multiversity, many units within the university stand alone, with little or no reliance on other units. These loose relationships with other organizational units within the institution are described by the term *loose coupling,* that is, the units are not tightly bound to one another in their everyday operations (Birnbaum, 1988). Here is an example. The division (or subunit) of student affairs attends to a variety of student needs through the provision of support services to undergraduate students, while the school of law is focused on educating graduate students for a particular profession. Also located nearby may be a research institute of physics. All of these subunits are vital components on which the larger university depends for its successful operation, but they rely very little (if at all) on one another for their survival or optimal performance. Nevertheless, these subunits may have strong relationships with audiences external to their university in order to carry out their work. This example illuminates the challenge in conceptualizing and studying a university's relationship with its surrounding community: it is highly fragmented, with many of its relationships existing between subunits and external constituencies.

Organizational learning literature explains that boundary spanning enables subunits to develop relationships or networks with audiences external to the university. Boundary spanning facilitates the movement of information between organization and environment, for if an organization is to gather information from its environment and have exchanges with other systems, then boundaries must be spanned. From an open systems perspective, boundaries exist, but they are often flowing and blurred (Scott, 1998), and community partnerships enable a university to begin to blur these boundaries. The ebb and flow and the complexity of information generated through partnerships at various levels of the organization—individual, program, or broader organizational level—allow the organization to remain healthy and responsive. Efforts to generate diverse community partnerships must take all of these organizational realities into consideration. In addition, to encourage the development of more networks and reciprocal flows of information and resources, partnerships should be inclusive of participants who are broadly representative of the constituencies within the university.

Recognizing and Tapping the Potential of Multiple Constituencies

Large research universities face challenges in creating a campus climate where all constituencies—faculty, students, and staff, as well as organizational subunits—hold a shared vision of their respective and collective leadership roles in furthering the broader university mission. Although the mission of the public research university is often described as research, teaching, and public service, this simplistic characterization can mistakenly lead to the assumption that all three mission components are easily defined, understood, and implemented. In fact, much discussion and even controversy often surround the interpretation of these terms and conceptions of the broader social utility of research, teaching, and public service. They are often seen as disconnected from one another, although proponents of an engaged institutional model would say that they are, in fact, one and the same. This is very much consistent with Boyer's view (1990) that faculty priorities should be reconceptualized to value not just discovery and teaching, but also the application and integration of knowledge. In other words, one's work should also reflect thoughtfulness about how knowledge will be practically applied.

Not surprisingly, much of the literature on the construction of a more engaged or responsive university focuses on faculty (Tierney, 1998; Boyer, 1990). Faculty clearly play a fundamental leadership role in guiding university practice and values, but there are other sizable constituencies within the institution as well. A learning organization stresses the importance of building capacity through maximizing the contributions of every constituent. The different roles historically ascribed to institutional constituencies (faculty, students, and staff) have had the effect of focusing engagement literature on certain institutional players (faculty) but not inclusive of all players. Renewed focus on how institutions serve society urges us to recognize all constituencies within the university as having a role to play in furthering these efforts. The learning organization requires the inclusion of all institutional members to maximize organizational capacity. Institutional engagement cannot be realized through a narrow focus on faculty roles in collaboration with the community or staff-run outreach programs, or through student volunteerism but rather through a process that is inclusive of all of these elements and encourages cross-collaboration among these constituencies. This holistic view of the institution and its multiple constituencies illustrates how it might more effectively leverage its resources to partner with communities.

When an institution and its members are urged to establish increased external networks through partnerships, it places on individuals the onus of representing the entire institution. Such a role can cause university representatives to embrace a shift in mind-set: they are no longer working in just their small subunit, which, for example, might focus on processing student financial aid; they are engaging in work that brings to bear the institution's overarching mission on their work with community members or groups. And while every individual within a university will not personally engage directly in work with the community members, embracing the concept of an engaged institution can be facilitated on a universitywide basis by adopting principles of the learning organization. The learning organization principles suggest that every individual is capable of tapping into her or his own abilities with her or his unique contribution producing organizational learning and ultimately increased capacity to carry out the institution's mission.

Research using organizational theory to guide, interpret, and study institutional efforts to be more engaged and responsive to their public, and in particular on promoting university and community partnerships, is rather limited. This chapter responds to the need to spur innovative thinking about both practice and research on engagement efforts by making a case for the adoption of a learning organization approach. Embracing the practice of institutional learning leads to both organizational processes and outcomes that are consistent with the model of an engaged institution. Within a context of increasing public and political expectations for more socially responsive, and therefore relevant, universities, such a framework is also argued to be of utility in studying institutional efforts to revitalize the mission of the public research university.

The remainder of this chapter focuses on key aspects of the learning organization and how they can be applied to enrich our thinking about organizational innovation, practice, and engagement in community partnerships.

Fostering the Learning Organization Through Community Engagement

Four key concepts from learning organizations are described in this section, with particular attention to their utility in stimulating organizational thinking about how greater emphasis on university and community partnerships might leverage university resources to develop an organization that is simultaneously engaged and learning.

The first of these concepts is *systems thinking,* which refers to the ability to recognize multiple layers and webs of interrelated actions (Senge, 1990). Some might break this down to more simplified terms: one looks at the big picture without losing sight of the brushstrokes. "Systems thinking is a conceptual framework, a body of knowledge and tools that has been developed . . . to help make the full patterns clearer, and to help us see how to change them effectively" (Senge, 1990, p. 7). To expand on an earlier example, those who work within the university may see the law school and the division of student affairs as two distinct subunits, and from an internal perspective, they would not judge either of their individual actions as representing the entire university. However, once the law school develops a relationship with an external actor, its actions are perceived as "the university's actions." In other words, the law school is now representing the entire university from an external actor's point of view. Therein lies a challenge: external audiences see the university as one single entity, while the reality within the institution is that its many subunits and individual actors are often highly fragmented and disconnected. Systems thinking is of particular interest in pushing forward our conception of the engaged institution, for it responds to the reality that an individual, programmatic, and institutional awareness, all embedded in a macrosystems perspective, is critical in the cultivation of community partnerships. It is the adoption of a systems perspective that allows institutional actors to understand the complex webs of interaction within the campus and to navigate them for the purpose of furthering institutional engagement with the community.

In my study of campus and community partnerships at one research university, a community partner explained the challenges inherent in initiating and sustaining relationships:

> Universities are labyrinths. . . . I know the university system really well and even at that, getting to the right person who's going to actually make a decision is difficult. You must have a centralized office or the community is going to be lost. . . . I have gotten to the point with some of our [other] universities where I am not going to be pushed and shoved from office to office anymore. I'm not going to put up with this. . . . And I am a tenacious individual [Anderson, 2004, p. 18].

This partner has his own experience with attempting to navigate the campus. His comments bring to the light the complex relationships present on a campus and the fact that even those who are internal to the campus can have difficulty in navigating these structures. Engaging in partnerships provides campus members the opportunity to view institutional complexity through the eyes of an outsider, so to speak, and to become more sensitized to structure and process. When institutional value is placed on increasing engagement and social relevancy of work, it can provide a shared vision of desired outcomes, which are navigated and made sense of through systems thinking. It can provide the individual a strengthened sense of his role and contribution to his personal work as well as institutional objectives.

Argyris and Schön (1996) posit that theories of action, which comprise norms, strategies, and assumptions, underlie all deliberate human behavior. They are applicable at the organizational and individual level and are described as ". . . including strategies of action, the values that govern the choice of strategies and the assumptions on which they are based" (p. 13). Two forms of theories of action are possible; espoused theory, which is used to justify a certain pattern of action, and theory-in-use, which is the actual theory implied by the actions taken (Argyris and Schön, 1996). The theories that are in use may deviate substantially from those that are espoused (Patriotta, 2003). In his work, Senge (1990) refers to theories-in-use as "mental models." This concept brings to the light the fact that at both the individual and organizational levels, the internal framework guiding actions must be identified, scrutinized, and, when necessary, reconceptualized. Individual recognition of one's theory-in-use requires a willingness to unearth what are often unquestioned assumptions about one's self and her beliefs about the organization.

In the case of university and community partnerships, individuals within the institution are challenged to reassess their own theories-in-use and the larger organization's espoused theory. For example, the mission of teaching, research, and service reflects an institution's espoused values. However, a faculty member's theory-in-use may place research at the forefront of her efforts with teaching and service as worthwhile but of lesser priority. Boyer's *Scholarship Reconsidered* (1990) challenges these theories of action at both the individual and institutional levels. His focus on integration and application, in addition to teaching and discovery, reflects a rethinking of the theories of action on which these practices rest. If individuals can shift their own thinking to construct a more integrated approach to teaching and research, there will be a shift in the nature of their work. Of course, this must be connected to an institution's espoused and in-use theories. In my study of partnerships, a community partner reflected on how an academic's theories-in-use regarding integrating and applying knowledge to real social issues can be affected:

> I think a lot of times what happens at the university level, and I could be wrong, is they talk about issues in the community without really knowing . . . without really having seen up close and personal what the issues are. I mean,

> I think it's easy through looking at statistics and through reading books and through reading a newspaper to come up with what they are, and I'm not saying they inaccurately do that, but I think there's a whole element that can be learned. . . . It can only come from being in the community and these organizations are access to the community . . . that's of tremendous value [Anderson, 2004, p. 24].

A faculty member also pointed out the utility of challenging one's theory-in-use and acknowledged the value of making knowledge more applicable to real-life situations:

> . . . intellectually, again, it provides a reality check. Another thing that it contributes . . . or reminds us is that also we have to translate what we talk about in theory into terms that make sense to people who don't deal with theory . . . being able to translate research into practice. . . . It's something that . . . it's not always easy to do and here is an opportunity to practice how to do that [Anderson, 2004, p. 22].

Engaging in partnership work requires an openness on the part of the participants to identify, challenge, and often alter their theories of action.

The concept of personal mastery is drawn from the work of Senge (1990), who argues that organizations learn to become learning organizations by relying on more than top-down expertise. In order to maximize their knowledge base, flexibility, and capacity for growth, organizations must encourage all individual workers to develop and deepen their own personal vision. Senge maintains that "the organizations that will truly excel in the future will be the organizations that discover how to tap people's commitment and capacity to learn at all levels in an organization" (p. 4). It is the sum of individuals' personal commitment and ability for learning that constitutes an organization's capacity. Personal mastery stresses the need for individuals to clarify what matters to them, focus their energies, and see the opportunities that lay before them objectively.

As Kezar points out in Chapter Four, Senge is unique in his inclusion of what have traditionally been recognized as nonrational processes as being critical for a sound learning process. Consistent with the work of individuals such as Gardner (1993), personal mastery embodies an expanded view of knowledge through its recognition of the value of creativity and intuition. It accounts for the fact that individuals bring their whole selves into their work and that often an organization benefits from individuals who are able to draw on their knowledge of self and others in order to work more effectively. Individuals cannot disconnect themselves from the need to make meaning out of their experiences. Fostering inquiry in the workplace highlights potential organizational rewards derived from tapping into the often underappreciated relationship between personal and professional satisfaction and organizational vitality. This individual commitment and engagement is foundational to the functioning of a learning organization. Due to the hierarchical organization of the university, most work on partnerships focuses on faculty or students (often relating to service-learning efforts), but staff are largely excluded. The concept of personal mastery is powerful because it ascribes to all individuals the potential to make meaningful contributions to the organization by applying and expanding their own personal range of knowledge. In essence, personal growth is recognized as optimizing organizational learning. By working to strengthen institutional engagement, both thinking and action relating to one's values, knowledge, and interests can serve to further collaborative work on community issues. As a faculty member explained of his work in the community,

> I am interested in this work because it meets certain values of mine in terms of giving care and expertise to families who simply wouldn't get it otherwise. . . . I have a personally meaningful relationship to people who are really doing what I think is valuable, mainly providing services to the families in our country that really do not have easy access . . . and we are doing frontier research [Anderson, 2004, p. 21].

A community partner similarly reflected,

> And so the fundamental relationship, I think, in terms of how a university interacts with the community is still personal. I think that you can have a department or a college or a school of a university foster a mission to interact with the community, but it still comes down to the imagination and determination of individuals [Anderson, 2004, p. 27].

Individuals are motivated by and committed to that which holds personal value. University and community partnership work provides opportunities to be creative about one's work while experiencing the satisfaction of combining one's professional role with other personal values.

A final concept of the learning organization is double-loop learning (Argyris and Schön, 1996). As Birnbaum (1988) notes, organizations can only respond to stimuli that they are designed to monitor; therefore, organizations must have sensors, or methods for detection of important information. In the process of cultivating community relationships, boundary spanning connects the university and community, but loops of learning specifically refer to the collection and use of information emerging from that connection. In the case of a single loop of learning, the gathered information is used to make adjustments as necessary to keep the organization functioning. There are no changes in organizational values or the theory-in-use; there is simply an adjustment in how a process is carried out. Morgan (1997) refers to double-loop learning as involving an additional step in this process that occurs when an issue is given a "double look" and adjustments are not just made automatically. The double loop allows for the questioning of whether operating norms are in fact legitimate and effective. Argyris and Schön (1996) point out that double-loop learning requires that individuals be willing to question their own assumptions and behaviors. If they are unwilling to honestly assess their theories-in-use, they will be largely blind to understanding how a shift in organization values or behavior might be necessary, thus preventing the process of double-loop learning. To engage in double-loop learning conveys receptivity toward more fundamental organizational changes if they are necessary. This requires that organizations have mechanisms to enact change and make adjustments if they are to effectively use the loops of learning.

The development of university and community partnerships signifies an initial step in seeking out external relationships, which will inevitably provide feedback to the campus partner and, ideally, the institution. Such information can be used to understand how the institution can be more responsive to community needs, but can also afford campus members a more active role as institutional representatives and actors in information gathering. One university partner explained the usefulness of the university's development of a center to promote partnerships:

> There are over 2000 projects here on campus that are doing something in the community. And . . . they don't know about each other. We feel like we're out there laboring all on our own, when right next door is another tutoring program that's serving little kids. . . . The University of California, Los Angeles Center for Community Partnerships has already played a powerful role in helping us to know each other better [Anderson, 2004, p. 24].

This illustrates how a loosely coupled organization can learn through the gathering of information and respond to it in order to function more effectively. This information can be used internally to inform the work of its center for community partnerships, with the outcome of increased clarity of partnership work and complex webs of interaction.

Conclusion

The application of a learning organization lens to the public research university reveals broad institutional benefits accrued through engagement in community partnerships. It is through such partnerships that the evolution of a more engaged and socially relevant institution might be nurtured. Adopting a learning framework can propel the shift in mind-set that is required for this purpose. The concepts of systems thinking, theories-of-action, personal mastery, and double-loop learning illustrate how increasing community engagement might, at the institutional level, infuse the entire university community with a new sense of purpose. At the individual level, pursuit of the institutional mission can be strengthened by empowering each individual with a sense of responsibility in making the learning organization wiser and more effective. The mission provides the "what," or the desired outcomes, of institutional learning, while the question of "how" to achieve this outcome is answered through the application of the concepts of the learning organization. A learning organization represents a process, a constantly thinking entity with the motivation and ability to respond to that information gathered from the environment.

This exploration of the research university as a learning organization illustrates one method by which institutions might reassess their true organizational capacity to engage in innovative practice that puts the ideal of the engaged institution into practice. Much is written of the value of, and need for, highly engaged universities that respond to societal needs, but it is also necessary that we begin to engage in thinking about how to fundamentally alter practice by putting to the test existing institutional theories of action. As one university partner explained, the time for this change is now, and partnership work is a natural mechanism for progress toward a more engaged institution:

> I think he's [the chancellor] smart enough to know that there's no longer just basic and applied research. There's this whole third category of engagement that is not the same as applied research. It's a way in which you can become better educated, not just in your discipline, but you can become a better person, you can become a better citizen, you can become a better leader. . . . I think he understands that there is a whole other dimension to knowledge generation and research, which is the moral and ethical dimensions of that knowledge and a way in which there is a public good to the generation and dissemination of knowledge . . . which has to be our focus because that's our identity as a research university [Anderson, 2004, pp. 27–28].

The task that lies before us is to continue to shift our thinking about how greater involvement in community partnerships can further the development of the engaged institution and how to provide every constituent within the university—students, staff, and faculty—a substantive role and responsibility in carrying this work forward.

References

Anderson, J. "Centralizing University and Community Partnerships at One Public Research University: An Organizational Analysis." Unpublished manuscript, 2004.

Argyris, C. *Reasoning, Learning and Action.* San Francisco: Jossey-Bass, 1982.

Argyris, C., and Schön, D. *Organizational Learning II: Theory, Method, and Practice.* Reading, Mass.: Addison-Wesley, 1996.

Birnbaum, R. *How Colleges Work.* San Francisco: Jossey-Bass, 1988.

Boyer, E. *Scholarship Reconsidered: Priorities of the Professoriate.* New York: Carnegie Foundation, 1990.

Boyte, H., and Hollander, E. *Wingspread Declaration on Renewing the Civic Mission of the American Research University.* Providence, R.I.: Campus Compact, 1999.

Braskamp, L., and Wergin, J. "Forming New Social Partnerships." In W. Tierney (ed.), *The Responsive University: Restructuring for High Performance.* Baltimore, Md.: Johns Hopkins University Press, 1999.

Cohen, M., and March, J. *Leadership and Ambiguity.* New York: McGraw-Hill, 1974.

Gardner, H. *Multiple Intelligences: The Theory in Practice.* New York: Basic Books, 1993.

Kerr, C. *The Uses of the University.* Cambridge, Mass.: Harvard University Press, 2001.

LeGates, R., and Robinson, G. "Institutionalizing University-Community Partnerships." *Journal of Planning Education and Research,* 1998, 17(4), 312–322.

Maurrasse, D. J. *Beyond the Campus: How Colleges and Universities Form Partnerships with Their Communities.* New York: Routledge, 2001.

Morgan, G. *Images of Organizations.* Thousand Oaks, Calif.: Sage, 1997.

Patriotta, G. *Organizational Knowledge in the Making: How Firms Create, Use, and Institutionalize Knowledge.* New York: Oxford University Press, 2003.

Scott, W. R. *Organizations: Rational, Natural, and Open Systems.* Upper Saddle River, N.J.: Prentice Hall, 1998.

Senge, P. *The Fifth Discipline: The Art and Practice of the Learning Organization.* New York: Doubleday, 1990.

Tierney, W. *The Responsive University: Restructuring for High Performance.* Baltimore, Md.: Johns Hopkins University Press, 1998.

Walshok, M. *Knowledge Without Boundaries: What America's Research Universities Can Do for the Economy, the Workplace, and the Community.* San Francisco: Jossey-Bass, 1995.

Weiwel, W., and Lieber, M. "Goal Achievement, Relationship Building, and Incrementalism: The Challenges of University-Community Partnerships." *Journal of Planning Education and Research,* 1998, 17, 291–301.

JODI L. ANDERSON *is a doctoral candidate in the division of Higher Education and Organizational Change in the Graduate School of Education and Information Studies at the University of California, Los Angeles.*

Instead of the traditional view of learning as acquiring cognitive knowledge or data, the author argues for a broader notion of knowledge that includes emotions, values, intuition, and creativity.

What Do We Mean by "Learning" in the Context of Higher Education?

Adrianna Kezar

Although many compelling studies have been conducted on organizational learning and the learning organization in recent times, most studies are built on a faulty assumption. The definition of learning within research on organizational learning and learning organizations is too narrow and has not kept pace with recent research on learning (Dierkes, 2001). In most scholarship on the learning organizations or organizational learning, learning is defined as knowledge or intelligence obtained through analysis or cognition; it excludes aspects such as emotions, creativity, and intuition. Also, learning and intelligence are defined, for the most part, as critical thinking represented through mathematical and linguistics knowledge, and the process of learning is also narrowly conceived as abstract reasoning.

In this chapter, I examine and challenge this notion of learning as falsely representing the process in nonholistic ways. I examine advances in our understanding of learning including research from psychology, cognition, and education on topics such as multiple intelligences, social and emotional components of learning, intuition, and creativity (Belenky, Clinchy, Goldberger, and Tarule, 1986; Gardner, 1993; Goleman, 1995; Klein, 2002; Salovey and Sluyter, 1997; Sternberg, 1999a). All of these critiques focus on an expanded view of the definition and process of learning.

Reexamining the definition of learning within this area of research is critical as society continues to diversify and become more global. We need to identify definitions of learning that embrace the growing diversity of people within institutions such as higher education. I believe that using the term *wisdom*, rather than *learning*, is important since learning has become associated with value-free, rational knowledge developed through abstract reasoning. Wisdom transcends various cultures and time periods and represents a broader definition. The dictionary defines *wisdom* as judgment, discernment and insight (often a spiritual orientation), reason (traditional notion of learning and knowledge), common sense (often normative or values driven), understanding (often through empathy and relationships), and perception (through experience and observation). I believe organizations that are wise are better situated to play a role in a multicultural and global world because they embrace a view of learning and knowledge that better reflects how these concepts are viewed internationally. I am not trying to dissuade readers of the importance of reasoning or concepts like systems thinking within organizations, but to reshape the notion of the learning organization and organizational learning so that it is a more powerful concept that can truly tap into the collective expertise of organizational members.

Theories of Knowledge

Two main theories of knowledge have guided research on organizational learning and the learning organization: rationalism and empiricism. Rationalism is a belief system that the truth or learning can be determined through "pure" abstract thought (Cook and Yanow, 1993). The world is made up of appearances, and our senses pick up on these and provide us with false information (and learning) that does not lead to knowledge (Varela, Thompson, and Rosch, 1991). We reach truth through our thoughts, not through our senses. Rationalism maintains that cognition is the processes of the mind that can be held to tests of truth (Sternberg, 1999a). Other processes of the mind that cannot be held to such tests are relegated to a different status, not part of cognition and not rational. Within rationalism, learning is focused on deductive reasoning, and knowledge becomes identified almost exclusively with logic and analysis that lend themselves more easily to such tests.

Empiricists (and later behaviorists) believe that reality lies only in the concrete world of objects that our bodies sense (Sternberg, 2000). We acquire knowledge through observation and experience. Empirical notions of learning and knowing shaped the behaviorists, who felt that we should study learning only in relation to behavioral change since consciousness could not be directly observed and could be studied only through introspection, an unreliable research tool. Also, learning became defined as changed actions or altered routines. J. B. Watson, B. F. Skinner, and Ivan Pavlov are the researchers most commonly discussed with behaviorist theories of learning.

Both rationalists and empiricists/behaviorists saw emotions, creativity, and intuition as aspects of the mind/body that prevented or clouded learning and knowledge development. The empirical and rationalist views were both influential to the development of the sciences and, later, social sciences. The result was that early research on cognition and learning focused on perception and observation skills, language development, and mathematical and logical reasoning almost exclusively (Sternberg, 2001). Learning was associated with cognition narrowly defined by processes that were believed to create verifiable knowledge. Since emotions, for example, were not seen as providing verifiable or testable information, it was not considered knowledge. Organizational learning theorists' work does examine the connection of values, emotions, and intuition to learning, but typically values are inhibitors rather than facilitators of learning. In terms of barriers, values and emotions are specifically seen as an impediment to the learning process.

Over the past century, several philosophies and theories (social constructivism, constructivism, and phenomenology) have challenged rationalist and behaviorist theories of knowledge and have shown them to have significant weaknesses (Stage, Muller, Kinzie, and Simmons, 1998). They have recently fallen out of favor, but outdated assumptions remain prevalent within the organizational literature.

Expanding Views of Organizational Learning and the Learning Organization

In the past thirty years, research from cognitive science has demonstrated that rationalist and behaviorist theories of learning are inaccurate and that an expanded definition of the product and process of learning is necessary. In this section, I review theories of multiple intelligences, social intelligence, intuition, and creativity as examples of this scholarship to demonstrate how views of the learning organizations and organizational learning might be expanded.

Theories of Multiple Intelligences and Learning. Although the mind has various functions (feeling, perceiving, memory), only reasoning has typically been associated with cognition and knowledge. The other functions might inform the reasoning process, but these functions alone were not capable of developing or central to reasoning or knowledge. Gardner (1983) launched one of the major critiques of the traditional view of knowledge as abstract reasoning represented through analytical and linguistic skills. After decades of cognitive research, he identified eight areas of intelligence: musical, bodily kinesthetic, logical-mathematical, spatial, linguistic, interpersonal, intrapersonal, and naturalist.

Like Senge's challenge of Western management, Gardner's theory challenges the traditional notion in Western societies that linguistic and logical intelligence, typically measured in IQ tests and associated with abstract reasoning, are the only intelligence of the brain. Western cultures have conceptualized the ability to see spatial patterns or read people's emotions not as intelligences but as talents or skills—not something to be nurtured by formal education and not something to be prized by society (but these are seen as intelligence within non-Western cultures). The contribution of

Gardner's theory is a pluralistic view of the mind; it invites us to recognize and nurture the varied human intelligences (Rosnow, 1994).

Sternberg (1999a, 1999b, 2000, 2001), another prominent scientist of cognition, also challenges the notion of intelligence as being predominantly associated with abstract reasoning processes such as logical and mathematical ability. He examines areas similar to those of Gardner such as analytical, practical, and creative intelligences. He found that people with high creativity and practical scores came from a much more ethnically and socioeconomically diverse group than those who scored on the traditional IQ-type measures. Sternberg argues, based on cross-cultural studies and failure of tests that try to identify a general intelligence, that there are various process skills such as practical, creative, and analytical that are part of a complex notion of intelligence. Analytical skills involve evaluation, judgment, and comparison, whereas creativity involves solving divergent and convergent problems, and practical intelligence is adaptation that people make to suit the environment.

Social and Emotional Intelligence as Learning. The notion that knowledge or intelligence can evolve from tapping into emotions is another concept that has typically been discounted by Western cultures and within the research on learning (Barret and Salovey, 2002). Emotional intelligence includes such abilities as knowing one's emotions and those of others, managing or regulating emotions, and assimilation of emotional experience into cognition and handling relationships. As noted by theorists of organizational learning, emotions typically cloud the development of knowledge. Organizational learning researchers reinforced the common wisdom that emotions lead to irrational and unwise information rather than knowledge.

Damaio (1994), Goleman (1995, 1998), LeDoux (1996), Salovey and Sluyter (1997), and Sternberg (1999a, 1999b, 2000, 2001) all review research from cognitive science that demonstrates that emotions and cognition are intertwined in order to support their view that emotional and social intelligence exists. Damaio (1994) studied patients with brain damage to their prefrontal-amygdala circuit (the site of emotions). He demonstrated that their decision making is flawed even though their cognitive or traditional IQ functions remain intact and argues that their decisions are so bad because they have lost access to their emotional learning. Cognitive science is building a strong case that feelings and emotions are indispensable for sound or wise decisions. Other researchers have investigated how various emotional states affect the process of learning and knowledge development (Claxton, 1999; Hogarth, 2001). People who are depressed have difficulty making decisions, while people in a positive mind-set tend to make better decisions. LeDoux experimented with rats by destroying their auditory system so they could not register sounds or learn from the "neocortex (site of cognitive processes), but the rats learned through an emotional reaction without any higher cortical involvement" (in Goleman, 1995, p. 18). The results of his studies demonstrated that what had been labeled the higher brain functions were not needed for learning. Emotions were found to be connected to the learning process and could in fact promote knowledge development independent of the higher brain function. This opened up a whole new area of research that had not been investigated before.

Intuition as Learning. Intuition has typically been defined as the ability to perceive possibilities, implications, and principles without being burdened by details and without conscious awareness (Hogarth, 2001, quoting Carl Jung). It is characterized by a lack of awareness of how outcomes have been achieved and can involve an interpretation of an event from the past or prediction into the future; it is usually based on context and observation. In many instances, the beliefs or predictions may not even be falsifiable. It is also important to social judgment and interactions, an area that has received less attention as important to intelligence.

Although there is no extensive body of research on intuition, a series of studies demonstrate that intuition can develop reliable decision making (Davis-Floyd and Arvidson, 1997; Klein, 2002; Laughlin, 1997). Other studies have shown that intuition is important to the development of knowledge in situations where there is ambiguity. Studies found that people depending on critical thinking skills were less likely to make successful decisions in highly ambiguous situations than people who used either intuition or creativity (Claxton, 1999). Certain professionals, such as surgeons, have also been studied since learning through formal reasoning (analytic principles of statistical decision making) was not as successful as educators had hoped (Monsay, 1997). Instead, they worked with surgeons to develop domain-specific knowledge through observation and apprenticeship and to tacitly develop intuition. The process was successful and led researchers to propose the importance of this type of learning for particular types of knowledge.

Klein (2002) studied intuition for over twenty years and established that intuition can lead to better decisions than critical reflection and analysis in some circumstances. In fact, analysis can get in the way of intuition, if people rely only on analysis and traditional methods of abstract reasoning for learning and knowledge development. He conceptualizes intuition as part of rational approaches to learning and knowledge development, trying to expand the definition of rationality rather than label intuition as an irrational process as it has been in the past.

Creativity as Learning. Studies have also been conducted on creativity and the way that it contributes to the development of knowledge (Craft, Jeffrey, and Leibling, 2001; Shaw and Runco, 1994). Creativity involves an imagining or seeing into the future; it is a capacity that helps to sort out a difficult situation and to plan how to tackle it. Similar to emotions, brain image mapping has found distinctive parts of the brain that control imagery, fantasies, and symbolization (Gardner, 1982). Gardner's research with brain-damaged patients demonstrated how they could lose artistic skills or maintain them even though other major brain functions, such as language, were lost. Studies by Taylor demonstrated that imagination and visualizing had a positive effect on student performance on exams; thus, studies also illustrate that creativity is intertwined with reasoning (Claxton, 1999). Gardner notes that most studies of learning and development have neglected creativity: "Piaget (and other well renowned scholars) explicitly states he is not interested in creativity as it is usually defined, or in the arts" (1982, pp. 210–211). Gardner's research demonstrates that creativity and the arts can be developed (in contrast to previous perspectives that believed that some people are born creative and this capacity naturally unfolds) and should be part of formal educational processes.

In summary, our views of what people learn (often termed knowledge) have expanded vastly to include many areas previously ignored, such as emotional or social intelligence, creativity, and intuition. This research implies new ways to conceptualize organizational learning and the learning organization.

Developing the Wise Organization and Rethinking the Learning Organization

The wise organization would have some fundamentally different assumptions and operating principles from the learning organization. First, the organization would expand its view of information and knowledge to include creativity, intuition, interpersonal skills, emotional intelligence, and the like. Each of these perspectives would be seen as equally valid approaches for helping to understand organizational issues and developing knowledge. Higher education institutions have a long tradition of valuing abstract learning and pure reason. This might make the transition to the wise organization difficult. Yet the liberal arts curriculum that focuses on the importance of the whole person and includes music and art may be the tradition to appeal to as it has a long history in higher education. Many people believe that a liberal arts education is best for preparing people for life, and certainly the analogy of the importance of using the whole person in the workplace would resonate with individuals on many campuses.

Second, the criteria for hiring individuals and their orientation to their positions will need to be reconceptualized. Individuals within organizations have hiring biases that favor candidates with linguistic and mathematical knowledge for jobs and reinforce a narrow approach to learning and knowledge. Higher education may be at an advantage compared to other organizations since fields such as student affairs have tended to favor and foster social and emotional intelligence. Another area from which to draw expertise are faculty in the arts and humanities. Yet it must be admitted that often fields that are not considered purely cognitively oriented are marginalized; for example, student affairs is marginalized to academic affairs and the humanities to the sciences. Therefore, although there are individuals representing multiple intelligences, there is still a hierarchy of value of organizational knowledge for decision making.

Third, wise organizations would have mechanisms in place to foster multiple types of learning. Many organizational processes will need to be reexamined, such as the way meetings are structured, the use of retreats and other activities that are better for fostering creativity, and more unstructured time for insight and creativity to emerge. Again, higher education may be able to excel in this area. Faculty positions are constructed to foster autonomy and creativity in many institutions. Administrative positions should be reconsidered, allowing more unstructured time and time alone for intuition and creativity to be fostered. Many administrative and faculty meetings are dominated by argumentation; there are almost no opportunities for brainstorming. Bensimon and Neumann's book on redesigning collegiate leadership (1993) looks at team-based models of organization that focus the contributions of diverse members of the organization and different mental approaches to developing knowledge that include interpersonal and intrapersonal intelligence and intuition.

These changes are all reflective of changes needed to reorient the culture of campuses, realigning the underlying values and assumptions. The shift from a rationalist/empiricist view of learning to multiple intelligences is a fundamental change in beliefs. Change in people's worldviews and core assumptions are often the most difficult to make. The large size of many campuses, many different constituent and interest groups or subcultures, and the hierarchical tradition of devaluing social intelligence and creativity make this a formidable task (see Kezar, 2001, for ways to engage such complex approaches to change). In the end, the wise organization would look vastly different with a new culture, altered values and assumptions, a new hiring and orienting process, and modified structures and processes.

It is also important to examine how learning organizations might look different based on the new research rather than abandoning the idea of the learning organization. Within Peter Senge's model, the supremacy of systems thinking should be reexamined. Perhaps learning organizations should have a set of thinking skills—intuition, creativity, insight, meditation—that are fostered to increase learning and the overall intelligence of the organization. The notion of systems thinking as the cornerstone to learning should be challenged. This might present a challenge to many institutions of higher education that have long heralded pure reason. The notion of mental models or assumptions can be greatly enhanced by the new learning research. Senge (1990) notes how surfacing mental models has proven particularly difficult. The purpose of meditation and insight is often to allow internal assumptions to become clear. The rational process of inquiry and reflection of forcing ourselves to recognize assumptions has, according to Senge, proven difficult. Faculty and staff struggle to move beyond their particular set of assumptions. In addition, Senge describes the challenge of achieving a shared vision. One barrier to a shared vision is that many people within organizations feel that their ideas and insights are not valued. A broader view of learning respects the talents of more people and can lead to more common ground that may facilitate a shared vision. In higher education, where there are so many different campus cultures and constituents with very different talents, this issue is of particular significance.

One of the most important implications of the new research on learning is that it can enhance the performance of teams, an area that Senge noted was a weakness within most organizations and an underused resource of wisdom. Most higher education organizations rely heavily on teams (through committees and cross-campus councils and groups) for decision making, policymaking, planning, and almost all other campus functions. Team members can better understand each other's strengths and contributions with a broader notion of intelligence. Our preferred method for team or group work is a form of abstract debate and discussion. Newer learning theories and research on intuition and insight might suggest that these structures are not best suited to enable other forms of intelligence. Some teams begin their work together through ropes courses and activity-based structures. More experimentation in this area might yield better group learning. Some organizations have their teams center themselves through meditation and reflection before they begin work. How might team learning be improved by using reflection or meditation? Do teams need activities that bring them out to the site of their work? For example, if they are addressing a policy issue about student admissions, perhaps they need to talk with new students and visit the admissions office. Many learners need to situate their learning within the context being examined.

The emphasis on shared assumptions and of team members' visions' being aligned might prevent them from tapping into different modes of intelligence. Senge does warn about the dangers of groupthink, and his emphasis on suspending assumptions, on dialogue and listening over debate, and on the spirit of inquiry are likely to lead to greater appreciation of diverse perspectives. These principles are important ground rules for moving toward the wise organization. Senge summarizes the spirit of inquiry that can lead to a wise organization:

> When people in an organization come collectively to recognize that nobody has the answers, it liberates the organization in a remarkable way. Many people will say that once you recognize that you can never figure life out, you have denied rationality. But that's not true. You have simply recontextualized rationality. To search for understanding, knowing that there is no ultimate answer, becomes a creative process—one which involves rationality but also something more [p. 282].

It is that "something more" that helps to build the wise organization and that has been missing from conceptualizations of the learning organization.

In order to make this new type of organization come to life, we also need new research on other types of learning. For example, research on organizational wisdom in higher education could focus on other types of organizational intelligence than previously envisioned. Interpersonal intelligence is an overlooked factor that is important to overall organizational functioning and success. A related area would be what it looks like for a university to possess intrapersonal or interpersonal intelligences. Can a college, through knowledge of itself, be more productive and effective? How can it use knowledge of itself to improve functioning? Another line of inquiry might be about the mix of intelligence and the effect on the organization. For example, what would a campus look like that balanced right and left brain thinking or was able to tap into different styles? How does an organization foster an environment that capitalizes on learning that balances affective and cognitive parts of the brain? Also, old questions about learning might be enhanced with this new approach. What competencies (examining interpersonal intelligence or intuition) can schools or colleges learn in order to interact with central administration better? Can networks of department chairs or deans be useful in developing creativity to solve complex problems?

The work that has already been conducted on intuition needs to be replicated in the higher education setting. How can campuses capitalize on intuitive knowledge developed in the classroom setting and labs or in administrative crisis situations for furthering organizational knowledge? Intuition is widely written about as part of the scientific process, but it has not been studied empirically. We understand the importance of intuition to firefighters and surgeons, but we lack knowledge of how this is important to or fostered within other work settings. The American workplace has often been touted for being a place of innovation and creativity, but creativity remains undervalued and understudied. Creativity is an extremely important feature of work in the academy that needs attention as workplace problems are increasingly recognized as divergent and needing the attention of creative thinking. These are just a few examples of areas in need of future research.

Conclusion

Higher education needs to create organizational learning to face the myriad of challenges and to best serve students. As educators, we all know the value of learning, yet we struggle to make it happen within our own campuses. In this chapter, I have provided evidence about the ways that views of intelligence and concepts of learning have changed and propose how these new perspectives can be combined with the concepts within the learning organization and organizational learning to develop an even richer concept: the wise organization.

There are many benefits to expanding our views of intelligence and learning. Organizations that expand their views of intelligence are likely to have more effective and productive workplaces since they will be using the knowledge of eight parts of the brain rather than just two or three. By expanding formal and informal training to include areas such as honing intuition and expanding creativity, interpersonal, and emotional intelligence from more traditional topics such as data management, strategic planning, or uses of technology, the full talents of the workforce can be harnessed. From a session on interpersonal intelligence, employees can improve their skills in organizing groups, negotiating solutions, developing personal connections (empathy), and engaging in social analysis (insight into people's feelings, motives, and concerns).

As organizations become more diverse and multicultural, the limited views of learning will likely inhibit organizations such as colleges and universities from capturing the collective intelligence of individuals who are part of cultures that value learning beyond linguistics and logic, as well as individuals in this culture whose talents have been devalued. An expanded definition of learning might create a greater sense of equity and inclusion within organizations. For example, individuals who feel their talents are marginalized in environments that reward only abstract reasoning may feel a greater commitment to an organization that embraces multiple forms of intelligence and learning. Equity is a moral imperative, but it also has tangible effects, such as increased morale, less absenteeism, and other rewards for organizations that choose this approach (Cox, 1993). The time seems right to move toward a more inclusive definition of learning within organizations. There is recognition that the context has become more complex and diverse.

References

Barret, L., and Salovey, P. (eds.). *The Wisdom in Feeling: Psychological Processes in Emotional Intelligence*. New York: Guilford Press, 2002.

Belenky, M., Clinchy, B., Goldberger, N., and Tarule, J. *Women's Ways of Knowing*. New York: Basic Books, 1986.

Bensimon, E., and Neumann, A. *Redesigning Collegiate Leadership*. Baltimore, Md.: Johns Hopkins University Press, 1993.

Claxton, G. *Wise Up*. New York: St. Martin's Press, 1999.

Cook, S., and Yanow, D. "Culture and Organizational Learning." *Journal of Management Inquiry*, 1993, 2(4), 373–390.

Cox, T. Jr. *Cultural Diversity in Organizations*. San Francisco: Berrett-Koehler, 1993.

Craft, A., Jeffrey, B., and Leibling, M. *Creativity in Education*. New York: Continuum, 2001.

Damaio, A. *Descartes' Error: Emotion, Reason, and Human Brain*. New York: Grosset/Putnam, 1994.

Davis-Floyd, R., and Arvidson, P. (eds.). *Intuition: The Inside Story*. New York: Routledge, 1997.

Dierkes, M. *Handbook of Organizational Learning and Knowledge*. New York: Oxford University Press, 2001.

Gardner, H. *Art, Mind, and Brain: A Cognitive Approach to Creativity*. New York: Basic Books, 1982.

Gardner, H. *Frames of Mind*. New York: Basic Books, 1983.

Gardner, H. *Multiple Intelligences: The Theory in Practice*. New York: Basic Books, 1993.

Goleman, D. *Emotional Intelligence*. New York: Bantam Books, 1995.

Goleman, D. *Working with Emotional Intelligence*. New York: Bantam Books, 1998.

Hogarth, R. *Educating Intuition*. Chicago: University of Chicago Press, 2001.

Kezar, A. *Reconceptualizing and Guiding Change in the Twenty-First Century*. Washington, D.C.: ASHE-ERIC, 2001.

Klein, G. *Intuition at Work*. New York: Doubleday, 2002.

Laughlin, C. "The Nature of Intuition: A Neuropsychological Approach." In R. Davis-Floyd and P. Arvidson (eds.), *Intuition: The Inside Story*. New York: Routledge, 1997.

LeDoux, J. *The Emotional Brain*. New York: Simon & Schuster, 1996.

Monsay, E. "Intuition in the Development of Scientific Theory and Practice." In R. Davis-Floyd and P. Arvidson (eds.), *Intuition: The Inside Story*. New York: Routledge, 1997.

Rosnow, R. "Intelligence and the Epistemic of Interpersonal Acumen: Testing Some Implications of Gardner's Theory." *Intelligence,* 1994, *19,* 93–116.

Salovey, P., and Sluyter, D. *Emotional Development and Emotional Intelligence: Educational Implications*. New York: Basic Books, 1997.

Senge, P. *The Fifth Discipline*. New York: Doubleday, 1990.

Shaw, M., and Runco, M. *Creativity and Affect*. Norwood, N.J.: Ablex, 1994.

Stage, F., Muller, P., Kinzie, J., and Simmons, A. *Creating Learning Centered Classrooms: What Does Learning Theory Have to Say?* Washington, D.C.: ASHE-ERIC, 1998.

Sternberg, R. *The Nature of Cognition*. Cambridge, Mass.: MIT Press, 1999a.

Sternberg, R. "A Dialectical Basis for Understanding the Study of Cognition." In R. Sternberg (ed.), *The Nature of Cognition*. Cambridge, Mass.: MIT Press, 1999b.

Sternberg, R. (ed.). *Handbook of Intelligence*. New York: Cambridge University Press, 2000.

Sternberg, R. *Complex Cognition: The Psychology of Human Thought*. New York: Oxford University Press, 2001.

Varela, F., Thompson, E., and Rosch, E. *The Embodied Mind: Cognitive and Human Experience*. Cambridge, Mass.: MIT Press, 1991.

ADRIANNA KEZAR is associate professor at the University of Southern California in the Higher Education Administration Program.

5

Knowledge management is defined and compared to information management and the institutional research function. In order to promote learning, new tools such as learning histories are needed, mistakes must be valued, and dissatisfaction recognized as part of the learning process.

Organizational Learning Through Knowledge Workers and Infomediaries

John Milam

Knowledge management (KM) is difficult to define, and although its attraction for business receives much attention, its implications for higher education are not clear (Thorn, 2001). The term *knowledge management* is used in different ways and is sometimes confused with *information management* (IM; Kay, 2000; Roell, 2004). Bernbom defines KM as the "discovery and capture of knowledge, the filtering and arrangement of this knowledge, and the value derived from sharing and using this knowledge throughout the organization" (2001, p. xiv). It is this "organized complexity of collaborative work to share and use information across all aspects of an institution which marks the effective use of knowledge" (Milam, 2001a, p. 1).

Knowledge starts as data, which include facts and numbers. "Information is data put into context. . . . Only when information is combined with experience and judgment does it become knowledge" (Kidwell, Vander Linde, and Johnson, 2000, p. 29). Knowledge is described as a dichotomy between explicit knowledge, which may be codified, packaged, transferred, and communicated, and tacit knowledge, which is more personal, context specific, and informal. This is why storytelling is an important tool in KM. Narrative describes action and images to convey complex, hidden meanings and tacit knowledge. As phrased by Agatha Christie in her 1942 novel *The Moving Finger*, "How much do we know at any time? Much more, or so I believe, than we know we know!" (cited in Landauer and Dumais, 1997).

Knowledge assets within an organization are not measured just by employees' skills, work processes, education, or experience but by their "capitalization as members of an organization" (Strassman, 1999, p. 14). KM strategies typically focus on best practices, training, customer relations management, business intelligence, project management, document management, search engines, the use of taxonomies, data warehousing, and supply chain management. The tasks of KM involve cultivating, nurturing, and exploiting knowledge at both the personal and organizational levels to help get the right knowledge to the right people at the right time (Oliver, Handzic, and Van Toorn, 2003).

Higher education institutions have "significant opportunities to apply knowledge management practices to support every part of their mission," explain Kidwell, Vander Linde, and Johnson (2001, p. 24). However, there are few examples of institutions that use "knowledge management as a way to operate" (Graham, 2001, p. 11). While there is a "high level of awareness" of the importance of KM in universities, research suggests that there is a "low level of actual implementation" (Oliver, Handzic, and Van Toorn, 2003, p. 143).

This chapter provides an overview of KM within the context of higher education.

Understanding Knowledge Management

A great deal of confusion exists about the meaning of the terms *knowledge* and *information*. Some practitioners argue that KM is nothing new; it is simply a reworking of library science and IM. Where IM is focused on storing and retrieving information, KM is more concerned with organizational outcomes. KM strategies move beyond disseminating knowledge to sharing and using it, especially within a community of practice (Bouthillier and Shearer, 2002).

As knowledge is identified, captured, and codified, it moves from something that is bound to human beings to something assimilated as objects of learning. As Roell (2004) explains, "Once it is 'explicated', it becomes information" (p. 2). The real work of knowledge is "mostly invisible," and its "observable end-products such as reports or decisions do not show from what process they have emerged" (p. 4).

Information Overload. The problem of information overload is both organizational and personal. Many employees are "awash in rising tides of content and data" and "waste many hours searching for, sorting, and assessing information, incurring a significant organizational productivity cost" (Rao, 2003, p. 29). It is very difficult to find relevant information quickly because it involves "digesting poorly or apparently featureless piles of documents. Thus, organizations don't draw on reservoirs of information that could influence a particular decision, task, or project. Ultimately, this leads to uninformed decisions, overlooked risks, and lost opportunities" (p. 29).

Knowledge as Competitive Advantage. Drucker (1995) explains that knowledge is the key economic resource in learning organizations and the dominant source of competitive advantage (Stevenson, 2001). KM strategies help organizations retain expertise during downsizing and turnover in personnel. Delio explains that although "knowledge does not result in a physical product . . . it can yield demonstrable results" (2000b, p. 36). These include increased speed of processes, improved quality, better customer service, and rapid innovation.

The Function of Institutional Research

There are numerous processes in higher education that involve a sustained and thoughtful commitment to organizational learning; among them are accreditation procedures, national association activities, the search for best practices, governance structures, quality improvement initiatives, accounting standards, and program review. There is a strong focus at many schools on improving key performance measures such as student persistence and engagement. In this era of public accountability and budget shortfalls, there are extensive efforts to measure institutional effectiveness and document the efficient use of scarce resources.

The functions of institutional research (IR) and assessment are usually considered central to these efforts. However, the IR function can be difficult to understand. It may be centralized or spread throughout an institution, and it is not always labeled as such (Muffo and McLaughlin, 1987). Knight (2003) explains that "despite the maturation of the profession, the question 'What is institutional research?' seems to be perpetual" (p. vi). Although "there is no consensus definition (or single reality) of what institutional research is," there is recognition that it is a "dynamic profession" that is "changing and expanding" as a "significant administrative support function on most postsecondary campuses" (Howard, 2001, p. v).

IR covers the "full spectrum of functions (educational, administrative, and support) occurring within a college or university" in "their broadest definitions" to support decision making (Middaugh, Trusheim, and Bauer, 1994, p. 1). It is tasked with collecting, extracting, editing, analyzing, and presenting information and data about enrollment, finance, courses, admissions, facilities, peer institutions, human resources, and assessment for management decision making. There are many tools and products of IR, including print and electronic fact books, data-driven Web sites, online surveys, data marts, data warehouses, interinstitutional data exchanges, online work flow applications, executive information systems, digital dashboards of performance indicators, and other types of attention management systems (Borden, Massa, and Milam, 2001).

The Role of Infomediary. IR professionals are comparable in many ways to what Costello (2000) terms "infomediaries" in KM. The infomediary "creates or manages systems to connect employees with the knowledge they need" (p. 33). While they "may bear any of a range of titles and may not be designated on the org chart as knowledge controllers," these knowledge workers "keep their finger on the pulse of the knowledge flowing around the organization" (p. 33).

The Changing Nature of IR. Borden, Massa, and Milam (2001) define the skills needed for the changing profession of IR as managing information flow, operating system competency, software application competency, systems planning and management, administrative systems, and information design. Perhaps the most critical, managing information flow, involves "the contextual grasp of how data and information enter the realm of institutional research and flow through storage, analysis and processing, output (as in reports) and into new storage" (p. 16). The transformation of IR through KM is discussed in greater depth by Serban and Luan (2002) and Milam (2001b).

Despite rhetoric to the contrary and the somewhat obvious parallel to KM, most IR offices are not seen as vital to their institutions but as an appendage. They represent a function mandated by federal and state law and, in some regions accreditors, to comply with guidelines for institutional effectiveness. Although there are notable exceptions, such as Alverno College for assessment, Johnson County Community College for IR at two-year colleges, Arizona State University and the University of Arizona for data warehousing, and Cabrillo College for data mining, the impact of IR at a high level of decision making is often minimal. (See Luan, 2003, for a discussion of data mining in higher education, which "has quickly emerged as a highly desirable tool for uncovering hidden patterns in vast databases and predicting.") There are, however, a growing number of presidents with IR backgrounds.

In order for institutions to move forward in their use of KM for more than traditional IR and IM, these roles and responsibilities must be turned upside down to view them from an entirely different perspective. Recognizing that most KM initiatives do not start at the top (Delio, 2000a), IR professionals are uniquely positioned to be the grassroots leaders of KM. Most other midlevel managers are bogged down in the day-to-day work of operations management. The critical question to ask is, "What can facilitate this change?" The answer is not to be found in better marketing of the IR profession; in attracting more administrators to the professional development activities of the Association of Institutional Research, although this is welcome; or in rethinking IR in terms of KM. There is a much larger problem: the need for a new type of dynamic organizational learning that occurs through transformation and personal change.

IR must be thought about differently in terms of how it can help serve new types of learning at the organizational and personal levels. The important lessons that may be learned through IR involve more than documenting the flow of information. New tools such as learning histories are needed that address the problems and inefficiencies within an institution. In order to get at this deeper and more powerful type of learning, personal change must take place, and organizations must undergo a radical transformation in how they share and leverage knowledge as an asset. As the following discussion will show, it is not enough to maintain the status quo of administrative information systems and IM.

Being Uncomfortable and Learning Through Transformation

"All learning is not the same; some learning is dysfunctional, and some insights or skills that might lead to useful new actions are often hard to attain" (Nevis, DiBella, and Gould, n.d., p. 2). Based on the work of Lewin, Schein (1995) explains that "all forms of learning and change start with some form of dissatisfaction as frustration generated by data that disconfirm our expectations and hopes" (p. 2).

While acceptable when voiced by students, there is little tolerance on campus for vocal dissatisfaction among faculty and staff. This would contrast noticeably with the public face that is presented to alumni, donors, and the larger community. Yet if administrators look closely at the data and information prepared by institutional research and assessment staff, there is much to be dissatisfied about. The percentage of minority faculty is often too low compared with the student population, and the attrition rate of minority students is too high. Graduation rates are far lower than desired at many institutions. Faculty salaries by discipline differ significantly by gender, and new employees are predominantly white male. Many students change majors, resulting in fewer minorities and women entering science and engineering fields than hoped for.

If one values dissatisfaction as necessary to organizational learning, then some form of disconfirmation starts to take place when these numbers are faced for what they say about colleges and universities. The status quo is then disrupted, possibly motivating people to change. Rather than merely being unhappy about performance measures in an equity scorecard, administrators must be so dissatisfied that they cannot tolerate further inaction.

Change is discussed at length in the higher education literature through a variety of lenses. In terms of learning for KM, what is important is for faculty and staff to recognize that the feelings of being uncomfortable and dissatisfied with the data about their institution are normal and necessary. They are a necessary part of the process. The natural tendency toward homeostasis must be resisted.

Valuing Mistakes. Senge (n.d.) explains the value of mistakes: "If we admit to ourselves and others that something is wrong or imperfect, we will lose our effectiveness, our self-esteem and maybe even our identity. Most humans need to assume that they are doing their best at all times, and it may be a real loss of face to accept and even 'embrace' errors" (p. 3).

Despite their commitment to promoting student and adult development, colleges and universities do not necessarily promote the kind of psychological safety that faculty and staff need to overcome the anxiety brought about by recognizing and valuing mistakes. Roth and Kleiner (1995) explain how "a corporate culture should be cultivated in which admitting and publicizing mistakes is seen as a sign of strength" (p. 5). Few want to admit that a valued intervention, especially one that involved a noticeable investment of time and resources such as a risk identification system for first-year students, has had little impact. This kind of insight often gets buried with a myriad of unanswered questions or with criticism over the use of methodology in the conduct of the institutional research. This is the "kill the messenger" reaction to institutional research, which works against what is a difficult and painful change process.

Unfortunately, a compliance mentality among administrators drives their use of institutional research. IR staff are used to complete mandatory paperwork. Managers are overwhelmed with their own personal KM problems and because of this do not always take the time to ask tough questions about data until there is a problem. Where there is a determined interest in improving a specific performance measure, this occurs because of a new state report, national commission study, or media scrutiny. Internal tracking systems such as affirmative action reports about hiring statistics are designed primarily to satisfy federal and state regulations and simply monitor compliance, not address how to fundamentally change the results. Because of this, they have little net impact on equity.

The management philosophy that many administrators hold makes it "harder for employees to be good learners and sharers" because staff "fear being penalized for revealing mistakes or seeking help" (Sugarman, 2001, p. 2). There is a tacit norm about not bringing up unresolved problems. Institutional researchers are often viewed as the harbingers of bad news instead of as a source of information for change.

Within many types of organizations, personnel have "naturally concealed their problems, reporting nothing, until they were close to a solution" (Sugarman, 2001, p. 2). In order to be more creative, managers and staff must discover and test their mental models and go through "significant personal change" (p. 3).

The Problem with Short-Term Fixes. Most organizations have a preoccupation with incremental improvement and trying to do things a little bit better (Roth and Kleiner, 1995). There is also an emphasis on obtaining short-term results, which is contradictory to the long-term work of process improvement. Managers task IR offices with finding out why a performance measure makes the institution "look bad," wanting them to find the "right data" that will "explain away" the problem.

One example of this phenomenon is space utilization. Classroom use may average thirty hours per week per room, but there is a perception of overcrowding and the need for more space. IR offices are asked to "improve" the utilization rate. While professional ethics preclude outright misrepresentation, additional data can be found through weekend use of space for noncredit activities such as CPR training and meditation classes. If these noncredit courses are counted, as reporting specifications permit, the utilization rate for classrooms can be increased to an acceptable level that does not raise alarms about inefficient use of space. Assumptions about preferred teaching times, student schedule preferences, and the prestige of priority scheduling are not addressed. The only thing that changes is the data for the performance measure.

In order to move beyond short-term, incremental fixes, a more transformational approach is needed. "This often means letting go of our existing knowledge and competencies and recognizing that they may prevent us from learning new things. This is a challenging and painful endeavor" (Roth and Kleiner, 1995, p. 5). Part of this difficult process involves critical self-reflection about one's own work and changing roles.

Sugarman (2001) describes a case study in organizational learning at a federal agency that addressed the problem of having a backlog of reports to produce:

> What led them to the solution was to question the real purpose for the reports. The breakthrough came when they realized that the reports were not an end in themselves, but a means to improve the quality and effectiveness of services to students with disabilities. By focusing on the results that mattered, on the true purpose of their program, they were able to view the problem in a totally different light. Once the problem was reframed, a solution that was previously inconceivable now became obvious. Stated with a little irony, the solution to having too many reports to produce was to produce fewer reports—because they saw that the reports per se did not really matter. What mattered was the corrective action that the reports were supposed to lead to— and there were more direct ways to get there [p. 19].

Senge (n.d.) discusses the work of Deming and the need for personal transformation that requires foundational changes in how we think and interact. This requires an appreciation of how organizational culture has become dysfunctional because of fragmentation, competition, and reactiveness.

The Problem of Fragmentation. Human beings are taught from an early age to break problems into pieces, yet this prevents us from seeing the increasingly systemic whole. There is a natural desire to separate organizational functions into walls and silos—for example, the distinction between academic and student affairs. Even natural opportunities for organizational learning, such as the release of an annual fact book, five-year program reviews, a schedule of board of trustees presentations, and annual affirmative action reports, are segmented by the perceived importance of the offices that prepare them. Rarely does the entire breadth of data and information across the institution get put into larger context.

At some times, silos of information are challenged with innovations such as an online program that requires new roles for faculty and new types and modes of delivery for student services. The "mental models that created the walls in the first place" must be challenged (Senge, n.d., p. 2). This example of virtual learning highlights how a systemic look at the institution is fragmented and compartmentalized. Data may be used for enrollment projections and space planning for the new program, but the impact on consumption of courses by virtual majors and the contribution of courses by departments is often overlooked, as are cost implications. Decisions are too often made in a vacuum because they are purposely kept insular.

The Problem of Competition. Competition in organizations often "makes looking good more important than being good. The fear of not looking good is one of the greatest enemies of learning" (Schein, 1995, p. 2). This environment encourages staff to work out problems in isolation in order to "protect ourselves from the threat and pain that come with learning, but also remaining incompetent and blinded to our incompetence" (p. 2). IR offices typically report to the vice president for finance or the chief academic officer function and work only within this sphere of influence, promoting another kind of silo. Cross-departmental collaboration is not always actively encouraged because of turf battles.

The Problem of Reactiveness. Senge (n.d.) explains how "we have grown accustomed to changing only in reaction to outside forces, yet the well-spring of real learning is aspiration, imagination, and experimentation" (p. 3). The reactive stance focuses on management by problem solving. In some ways, this is very much the male model of leadership. Whether it is a low rate of course completion, high faculty turnover, or a growing reliance on part-time instructors, administrators as problem solvers try to "make something go away" (p. 3) rather than understand all of the interrelationships between the issues.

Reactiveness usually takes place in an atmosphere of crisis. When a problem arises, IR offices are asked to quickly review the higher education literature, contact peer institutions to see how they addressed it, and compile a new report or white paper. A new committee or task force is charged with investigating the problem, gathering feedback from the community, and recommending solutions. These are standard approaches to organizational learning, which, despite the best of intentions, promote the status quo. Their inquiries and reports will not dramatically change or transform anything, and the net effect on relative performance measures will be minimal.

A higher order of organizational learning requires a very different mind-set. One KM tool that helps with this effort is the use of learning histories for storytelling. IR and assessment are central to telling these new kinds of stories.

Learning Histories and Storytelling

Part of promoting creativity is documenting what Roth and Kleiner (1995) call a "learning history." They argue that the measurement and assessment processes that occur in most business and governmental organizations, which are roughly comparable to the role of institutional research, are not appropriate rubrics for organizational learning. A more useful approach is to "capture and convey the experiences and understandings of a group of people who have expanded their own capabilities. The resulting document may become a new and much-needed form of institutional memory" (p. 2).

A learning history tells a story about how an organization learned something important through some kind of concerted effort. Rather than focus on incremental changes, the topic is usually one of transformation or reexamination of a pressing issue relative to performance. The resulting history can take many forms, including written documents and multimedia products. Whatever the form, it needs to describe the false starts and failures of how people tried to solve a problem and wrestled with the issues. The history is designed to bring out into the open all of the messy psychological and emotional problems encountered during the process.

Learning historians use qualitative research and ethnography to triangulate narratives, data, and interview results in order to ensure validity. Through the use of these histories, the focus shifts from finding solutions to promoting inspiration. This is comparable to qualitative assessment efforts such as interviewing first-year students and asking such questions as, "What stands out for you about your first year of college?" Grounded theory building and the emergence of themes are more important than documenting student success with quantitative measures. In learning histories, a naturalistic, constructivist perspective is used that involves "capturing and constructing stories, gathering data from a wide group of people so that judgments can be made about whether or not a story is typical" (Roth and Kleiner, 1995, p. 4). It is the honesty of these learning histories that lets people "speak more truthfully about underlying issues" (p. 8).

While the act of learning through reflection has its place, this process sometimes carries a burden or pressure to prove results or serve a political agenda. Instead of immediately trying to identify problems and look for solutions, uncertainty should be valued rather than be seen as a sign of indecisiveness. This new approach to learning "inevitably leads people to think about muddled, self-contradictory situations" (Roth and Kleiner, 1995, p. 5).

New Kinds of Learning Leadership

It requires courage and commitment by organizational leaders to value the difficult processes of writing learning histories, valuing mistakes, recognizing contradictions, and focusing on long-term solutions. This approach requires different skills and experiences in managing creativity. Institutional research and assessment must be viewed as integral parts of a new tool set.

Jaworski and Scharmer (2000) describe the importance of observing, sensing, knowing, crystallizing, and executing. Observing means "seeing reality with fresh eyes." Sensing involves recognizing and opening oneself up or "turning into emerging patterns that inform future possibilities." Knowing requires "accessing inner sources of creativity and will." Crystallizing means "creating vision and intention," and executing requires "acting in an instant to capitalize on new opportunities" (Scharmer, 2002, p. 2).

In the use of institutional research for organizational learning, sensing and knowing are particularly relevant. Scharmer (2002), cofounder of the MIT Leadership Lab, explains that sensing involves "paying attention to things you are normally not aware of: activities you perform by rote, inter-actions you take for granted, expectations you've never questioned, or meanings you've never explored. The more you succeed in suspending your habit of judgment about what you notice and observe, the more clearly you will see what is going on around you" (p. 3). Institutional researchers must be asked to go beyond the data and information they convey with routine and ad hoc reporting to examine larger questions. While short-term fixes such as increasing faculty out-of-class interaction with students can be put in place to try to increase a measure such as student engagement, the prob-lem of engagement is much more multivariate in nature than this type of simplistic innovation implies.

Knowing. Knowing involves asking, "What needs to be done here?" This involves telling stories with data to get at the heart of contradictions and dissatisfaction. Instead of being fixated with short-term solutions so as not to appear uncertain, intense questioning needs to be done, asking, "Who is my Self and what is my Work?" (Scharmer, 2002, p. 3). New infor-mation can then be synthesized and experiences analyzed until new insights begin to emerge through learning histories. IR staff are best positioned to serve as these new learning historians.

Presencing. Scharmer (2002) defines a new term, *presencing,* as "when the highest possible future that wants to emerge is beginning to flow into the now" (p. 3). Presencing involves paying close attention to the inner pro-cesses of thought. In preparing and using learning histories, this means let-ting oneself feel emotionally about the topic. It means questioning and examining every assumption about an IR issue, including beliefs about why graduation rates are low, what contributes to them, and attachment to cer-tain innovations or strategies despite the lack of data to support them.

Most theories of organizational learning build on Kolb's work about experiential learning, which promotes reflection about the past. This learning strategy does not go far enough to promote transformation, because "leaders cannot meet the challenges they face by operating on a past-driven learning cycle" (Scharmer, 2002, p. 3). Successful innovation and change depend not just on "what leaders do and how they do it, but the inner place from which they operate" (Scharmer, 2002, p. 3). The term *presencing* blends "pre-sensing" and "presence," placing an intense focus on attention.

With this new approach, presidents, chief academic officers, and other leaders use learning histories to tell the stories that need to be told, stories that strongly convey difficult and uncomfortable information and stir peo-ple to action. These stories let institutional leaders and managers confront problems and inefficiencies in new ways by focusing intensely on the thought processes involved, including the most basic and dearly held assumptions about their work and why they do it the way they do. These stories are not about the past but about seizing critical opportunities for change in the present.

Conclusion

KM requires a serious commitment to organizational change that comes through experimenting with new tools such as learning histories and storytelling and by challenging fundamental assumptions about the higher education enterprise. This is possible only if administrators are willing to tolerate being uncomfortable, dissatisfied, and uncertain and if they learn to value long-term processes over quick fixes and problem solving. Out of these shifts comes a new level of inner attention to thought: presencing.

While the description of this new type of KM leadership may seem far removed from the day-to-day business of higher education administration, this represents a pivotal choice for managers. Colleges and universities are complex, and their flow of information for operational decision making is adequate at best, even with the latest technology for attention management. The problems of information overload and lost productivity that occur because of inefficient searching for knowledge appear insurmountable. The reliance on strategies of information management takes institutions only so far.

While organizational learning appears at first to be widespread, this essential KM strategy is either dysfunctional or lacking. Many activities of institutional research, assessment, and institutional effectiveness appear to address this need, but only superficially. These staff roles need to be reconceptualized as "infomediaries" and charged with documenting the flow of hidden, tacit knowledge and organizational memory. However, this strategy is not enough in itself and gets only at the most basic layer of KM.

Institutions will fail to leverage the full potential of organizational learning unless they promote a climate where dissatisfaction and mistakes are valued, contradictions and conflict are welcomed as learning opportunities, and organizational change promotes transformation at the most personal level in how administrators, faculty, staff, and students use knowledge in a community of practice. The highest good of society's institutions of higher education will not materialize until this lesson in learning is understood and actualized.

References

Bernbom, G. (ed.). *Information Alchemy: The Art and Science of Knowledge Management.* San Francisco: Jossey-Bass, 2001.

Borden, V., Massa, T., and Milam, J. "Technology and Tools for Institutional Research." In R. D. Howard (ed.), *Institutional Research: Decision Support in Higher Education.* Tallahassee, Fla.: Association for Institutional Research, 2001.

Bouthillier, F., and Shearer, K. "Understanding Knowledge Management and Information Management: The Need for an Empirical Perspective." *Information Research,* 2002, 8(1). http://informationr.net/ir/8–1/paper141.html.

Costello, D. "For Knowledge, Look Within: Businesses Are Discovering the Value of Internal Infomediaries." *Knowledge Management,* 2000, 3(9), 33, 39–41.

Delio, M. "Grass Roots Are Greener: Knowledge Initiatives Advance from Bottom-Up Successes, Not by Executive Fiat." *Knowledge Management,* 2000a, 3(2), 47–50.

Delio, M. "Proving We're Productive." *Knowledge Management,* 2002b, *3*(7), 33–38.

Drucker, P. F. *Managing in a Time of Great Change.* New York: Penguin Books, 1995.

Graham, R. "Benchmarking Jackson State." *Knowledge Management,* 2001, *4*(5), 11. http://www.destinationcrm.com/km/dcrm_km_article.asp?id=829.

Howard, R. (ed.). *Institutional Research: Decision Support in Higher Education.* Tallahassee, Fla.: Association for Institutional Research, 2001.

Jaworski, J., and Scharmer, C. O. "Leading in the Digital Economy: Sensing and Seizing Emerging Opportunities." 2000. www.generonconsulting.com/Publications/Leading_in_the_Digital_Economy.pdf.

Kay, A. "By Any Other Name." *Knowledge Management,* 2000, *3*(7), 8. http://www.destinationcrm.com/km/dcrm_km_article.asp?id=336.

Kidwell, J. J., Vander Linde, K. M., and Johnson, S. L. "Applying Corporate Knowledge Management Practices in Higher Education." *EDUCAUSE Quarterly,* 2000, *4,* 28–33.

Knight, W. E. (ed.). *The Primer for Institutional Research.* Tallahassee, Fla.: Association for Institutional Research, 2003.

Landauer, T. K., and Dumais, S. T. "A Solution to Plato's Problem: The Latent Semantic Analysis Theory of Acquisition, Induction, and Representation of Knowledge." *Psychological Review,* 1997, *104,* 211–240.

Luan, J. "Data Mining: Predicting Modeling and Clustering Essentials: A Step-by-Step Manual." Association for Institutional Research preforum workshop materials, Tampa, Fla., 2003.

Middaugh, M. F., Trusheim, D. W., and Bauer, K. W. *Strategies for the Practice of Institutional Research: Concepts, Resources, and Applications.* Tallahassee, Fla.: Association for Institutional Research and North East Association for Institutional Research, 1994.

Milam, J. "Knowledge Management for Higher Education." In *ERIC Digest.* Washington, D.C.: ERIC Clearinghouse on Higher Education, 2001a. http://www.ericfacility.net/databases/ERIC_Digests/ed464520.html. (ED 464 520)

Milam, J. "Knowledge Management (KM): A Revolution Waiting for IR." Paper presented at the annual meeting of the Association for Institutional Research, Long Beach, Calif., June 2001b.

Muffo, J. A., and McLaughlin, G. W. (eds.). *A Primer on Institutional Research.* Tallahassee, Fla.: Association for Institutional Research, 1987.

Nevis, E. C., DiBella, A. J., and Gould, J. M. "Understanding Organizations as Learning Systems." Society for Organizational Learning, n.d. http://www.solonline.org/static/research/workingpapers/learning_sys.html.

Oliver, G. R., Handzic, M., and Van Toorn, C. "Towards Understanding KM Practices in the Academic Environment: The Shoemaker's Paradox." Academic Conferences Limited, 2003. http://www.ejkm.com/volume-1/volume1-issue-2/issue2-art13-oliver.pdf.

Rao, R. "From Unstructured Data to Actionable Intelligence." *IT Pro,* Nov.–Dec. 2003, pp. 29–35. http://www.inxight.com/pdfs/f6raolo.pdf.

Roell, M. "Distributed KM—Improving Knowledge Workers' Productivity and Organisational Knowledge Sharing with Weblog-Based Personal Publishing." Paper presented at Blog Talk 2.0, European Conference on Weblogs, Vienna, July 2004. http://roell.net/publikationen/distributedkm.shtml.

Roth, G., and Kleiner, A. *Learning About Organizational Learning—Creating a Learning History.* Cambridge, Mass.: MIT Center for Organizational Learning, 1995. http://www.solonline.org/static/research/workingpapers/18001.html.

Scharmer, C. O. "Presencing: Illuminating the Blind Spot of Leadership: Foundations for a Social Technology of Freedom." 2002. http://www.generonconsulting.com/Publications/PresencingIntro.pdf.

Schein, E. "Kurt Lewin's Change Theory in the Field and in the Classroom: Notes Toward a Model of Managed Learning." Society for Organizational Learning, 1995. http://www.solonline.org/static/research/workingpapers/10006.html.

Senge, P. M. "Personal Transformation." Society for Organizational Learning, n.d. http://www.solonline.org/res/kr/transform.html.

Serban, A. M., and Luan, J. (eds.). *Knowledge Management: Building a Competitive Advantage in Higher Education.* New Directions for Institutional Research, no. 113. San Francisco: Jossey-Bass, 2002.

Stevenson, J. M. "Modern Practice, Pragmatism, Philosophy in Higher Education Administration: Knowledge Leadership of the Chief Academic Officer." *College Student Journal,* June 2001. http://www.findarticles.com/p/articles/mi_m0FCR/is_2_35/ai_77399623.

Strassman, P. A. "What's the Worth of an Employee? Knowledge Capital Is an Attribute of Organizations, Not a Characteristic of Individuals." *Knowledge Management,* 1999, 2(12), 14. http://www.destinationcrm.com/km/dcrm_km_article.asp?id=155.

Sugarman, B. "A Learning-Based Approach to Leading Change: Five Case Studies of Guided Change Initiatives." Society for Organizational Learning, 2001. http://www.solonline.org/repository/item?item_id=360596.

Thorn, C. A. "Knowledge Management for Educational Information Systems: What Is the State of the Field?" *Educational Policy Analysis Archives,* 2001, 9(47). http://epaa.asu.edu/epaa/v9n47/.

JOHN MILAM is executive director of HigherEd.org, Inc., a consulting firm focused on knowledge management for higher education.

*What follows is the Portland State University story, a
reflection on change as a scholarly act within a learning
community using techniques from organizational
learning.*

Modeling Learning: The Role of Leaders

Judith A. Ramaley, Barbara A. Holland

This chapter explores the role of leadership during a period of transformational change. At Portland State University (PSU), major change has been a
constant feature of the institution's history. "From 1971–1974, there was
almost constant discussion of retrenchment, dismissals and budget reduc-
tions" (Dodds, 2000, p. 371). Dodds went on to name the period from 1974
to 1996 the "*second retrenchment era*" (p. 383). The most recent phase of
major retrenchment, which began in 1991, led to a major transformation
of the institution rather than a further diminution of its prospects. In this
chapter, we explore why this was so.

Academic organizations are often resistant to major changes. Yet
between 1991 and 1996 (the date of its fiftieth anniversary), PSU leadership,
faculty, students, and external stakeholders worked together to absorb serious budget cuts, redesign the undergraduate curriculum, revise the institutional promotion and tenure guidelines, and grow to become the largest
university in Oregon. To achieve such sweeping changes, PSU had to
develop a capacity to learn as an organization in order to guide and inform
change and come up with fresh strategies after the near exhaustion of so
many years of retrenchment and budget constraint. This chapter draws on
PSU experiences to describe a model for change through a focus on organizational learning and research. At PSU, change became the product of a
scholarly approach to institutional challenges.

The argument here is that deep and pervasive change can occur if both
the leader and the campus community define intentional change as a scholarly act strongly rooted in a culture of organizational learning. The leader
must assist in creating the characteristics and capacities of an organization

that can approach change in a scholarly way, that is, an organization that can learn in a manner legitimated and sanctioned by the academic disciplines from which its leadership and sense of professional identity are drawn. This conception has consequences for the part that individuals in the campus community will play and how they will relate to each other.

As Garvin (1999) has explained, the leader plays two related roles in creating the capacity for an organization to learn. First, to move a group of people into an inquiry mode, the leader must serve as a teacher. "To that end, executives are urged to share their distinctive perspectives about their companies' strategies, purposes and values. They are told to develop 'a teachable point of view' that captivates and enlightens, communicating it to employees through stories and parables" (p. 188). This advice is reminiscent of the way Gardner describes innovative leadership: "The innovative leader takes a story that has been latent in the population, or among the members of his or her chosen domain and brings new attention or a fresh twist to the story" (p. 10). Leaders who tell good stories can give purpose and meaning and ensure cohesiveness in a group.

By itself, however, teaching is not enough. The leader must also lead learning: "New ways of thinking become the desired ends, not facts and frameworks. Discussion and debate replace *ex cathedra* pronouncements. Questions become as important as answers" (Garvin, 1999, p. 189). At PSU, the role of the president in this process was to teach and foster learning. In describing the characteristics of a learning organization, Senge (1990) identified five disciplines. The PSU story illustrates all five of these disciplines: systems thinking, personal mastery, mental models, building a shared vision, and team learning. The first four disciplines are needed to undertake meaningful change. To move beyond the first stage of systemic change, we must invoke the fifth discipline, which is team learning.

The overall goal of the leader in a scholarly change process is to set up the capacity to frame important questions that will affect the trajectory of the organization and foster a scholarly approach to managing these questions. This requires a network of communities of practice and support for their ongoing process of discovery. A campus can learn to identify and use its tacit knowledge as well as the explicit knowledge of each field in an integrative way. Thus, the organization takes an active approach to knowledge management and creates a sustained capacity for learning.

The Portland State Story

In this story we demonstrate some of the barriers and facilitators of organizational learning and the role leaders play in overcoming these barriers.

The Influence of Historic Claims. As we explore the lessons that can be learned from the experience of PSU, imagine for a moment the context in which the story began. In 1990, a new president arrived on campus after the unhappy departure of her predecessor; the institution held competing views of its mission; the community longed for the symbolism and substance of a major university in the Portland metropolitan area; the resource base available to the institution and to the Oregon state system was about to be radically reduced because of a tax reduction measure; and the institution itself had low expectations of its future and its fortunes after enduring repeated periods of retrenchments and dashed hopes (Dodds, 2000). The arrival of a new president created the possibility of a new way of seeing things, and the prospect of dramatic budget cuts made it mandatory for the institution to rethink its mission, core competencies, and community relationships.

The process of building a scholarly case for action (it's a warrant) is complex (Mark, Henry, and Julnes 2000). It starts with a claim (that a particular condition exists, that something has value, that a particular action should be taken), builds evidence to test and support the claim, establishes a warrant (a statement justifying the evidence that serves as a basis for a particular claim), and carefully spells out any qualifications for the claim (the specific circumstances under which a claim may be true and the likelihood that it is true). A warrant involves a complex interweaving of evidence, explanation, and clearly articulated values (House and Howe, 1999). At PSU, we began by examining and challenging the historical and constraining claims. Through a combination of intentional strategies and happy accident, we exposed the fallacies of the initial claims of constraint and poverty that had paralyzed institutional spirit and optimism. This initial "unlearning" was critical to creating the capacity for new organizational learning.

We reframed our challenges by basing our case for change on academic values, not administrative ones. Wilson (1989, p. 91) has argued that "every organization has a culture, that is, a persistent, patterned way of thinking about the central tasks of and human relationships within an organization." Often an organization harbors several different cultures. Within the academy, administrative and faculty cultures are distinctive in their decision-making conventions, time frames, priorities, and constituencies (Martin, Manning, and Ramaley, 2001). Any approach to meaningful change must start from a common set of values that can make the divisions of administrative and academic culture less formidable. Since the core of academic life is scholarship, why not adopt a scholarly mind-set and standards of scholarly excellence as the tests of a good warrant for change?

Avoiding Decision Traps. In times of crisis or emergency, it is easy to make some serious mistakes in putting together a warrant. The PSU story is, at its heart, about how we avoided those traps. The experience also sheds some light on the challenge of leadership in a time of change. The basic role of leadership at any time, but especially during periods of abrupt and unanticipated change, is to help the institution avoid the pitfalls of what Russo and Schoemaker (1989) call "decision traps." Consistent with academic culture, a leader must model a scholarly and principled approach to decision making, guided by a clear and shared vision of the institution (Ramaley,

2000). The purpose of behaving in a scholarly way and according to high standards of scholarship is to create a strong warrant for action, based on the discipline of inquiry with which accomplished scholars are familiar.

First, let us consider the most common decision traps, drawing liberally on Russo and Schoemaker (1989) but adapting their ideas for these purposes. What follows is a list of aspects of decision making where errors are frequently made:

Framing the question: Setting out to solve the wrong problem because you have a mental framework for your decision that causes you to overlook the best options or lose sight of the problem you really need to solve.

Taking time to assess your current situation: Plunging in without taking time to think about the crux of the issue you are facing or to think through how you would like decisions of institution-shaping magnitude to be made.

Approaching the challenge from a scholarly perspective: Being overconfident in your own judgment and knowledge and failing to collect needed information because you are too sure of your own assumptions and opinions. We think we know, in other words, why things are the way they are; however, what we know is often wrong.

Learning from experience: Failing to pay attention and keep track of what happens so that you have a record you can study and interpret in order to draw lessons from your experience. This step, which is often neglected, is an important component of the leadership of change. Change can set in motion reactions that ripple out in unpredictable and unanticipated directions. Thoughtful and well-grounded adjustments in strategy are often needed to accommodate these reactions and unintended consequences.

How did we avoid all those pitfalls? The key ideas that set the stage for the transformation of PSU that exists today were simple but powerful. In *framing the question,* we figured out that our challenge in 1990 was not about how to cut the budget. The core question was how to spend wisely the budget we were likely to have, whatever it was going to be, in order to move toward a vision of ourselves as an urban research university. We took *time to assess our current situation* in order to test more carefully the various claims that had been made about our students and their achievement. As we began this exercise, we were well aware of our poor retention and graduation rates, but we assumed this was due to our status as an urban institution with a predominantly part-time, commuting student body, many of whom had begun their postsecondary education elsewhere and most of whom faced serious obstacles on their way to achieving their educational goals. When we looked closely at why we had such low retention and graduation rates, we were surprised. When we exchanged data with institutions with a similar mission and a comparable student body, we learned that most of them had much better retention and graduation rates than we did. We reasoned that our problems were not caused by our location or our students' traits. Further reflection and study revealed that our problems stemmed from the fact that we did not have a coherent educational philosophy or a way to create a community of learning for either our students or faculty.

To acquire the capacity to articulate and achieve a distinctive sense of mission and educational philosophy, PSU had to answer two basic questions. First, we had to figure out what we wanted to *be*. Then we could work on what we wanted to *do* to handle our budget crisis and create the competencies we would require to take us toward the future we wanted. Most important, we had to do that together. Fortunately, PSU had a tradition of cooperation between faculty and administration, learned through many bouts of painful retrenchment (Dodds, 2000).

What we wanted to be focused on next was our educational approach and the design of our curriculum. Our aspirations as an urban research university meant that we had to address the core of our historic purpose: access to learning and knowledge generation focused on the urban experience. We created a new motto: Let Knowledge Serve the City (*Doctrina Urbi Serviat*). From the beginning, we approached our challenge from a *scholarly perspective*. We set out to learn what we needed to know to develop a curriculum and an institutional mission and identity based on a clear vision of what it would mean to be an educated person in the twenty-first century. For PSU, change became a scholarly act. This required some basic administrative changes, but the dominant force was a set of well-warranted educational ideas based on a careful study of the research then available on the undergraduate experience and its applicability to our institution and students. Those ideas had power and led us to a vision of what we wanted to do: become an urban research university with an innovative curriculum designed primarily for nontraditional students that integrated teaching and research into new forms of engaged scholarship and engaged learning. Administrators and faculty used a scholarly approach to collaborate in decision making on critical issues. What follows is a model for large-scale change that emerged from that experience.

The value of thinking about change as a scholarly approach to developing a warrant led us to build in the opportunity to *learn from experience*. A scholarly approach requires continuous gathering of data, interpretation of the results of various changes at the institution, and an infrastructure to allow faculty and staff to develop the knowledge, skills, and dispositions needed to work together in a scholarly mode about the institution and the curriculum. The infrastructure need was addressed by the formation of the Center for Academic Excellence, a faculty-led support model that invests in design and evaluation of educational experiences and faculty development opportunities. The center proved invaluable in creating capacity for creative change and the sustainability of innovations.

Large-Scale Change as a Scholarly Act

Transformational change must be deep, pervasive, and continuous (Eckel, Green, and Hill, 2001). The experience of change of this kind gradually alters the shared expectations, culture, habits of mind, and ways of doing things (Ramaley, 2002).

There are many ways to think about large-scale change and to model its stages and underlying structure (for example, Heifetz, 1993). In describing the experience of PSU, we elected to combine several of these models into a single five-element framework (Ramaley, 1996): (1) building a compelling case for change, (2) creating clarity of purpose, (3) working in a scholarly mode at a significant scale, (4) developing a conducive campus environment, and (5) understanding change.

Building a Compelling Case for Change. A core challenge was to get past the historic assumption of inescapable impoverishment and demonstrate that it was possible to make changes without the infusion of major new financial resources. The need for deeper and more pervasive change can be triggered by external mandates, fiscal crises, internal problems like our poor retention rates in those days, or a desire to prepare for the future. At PSU in 1990, all of these forces were active at once. Depending on the energy and imagination of a campus community, reactions to these forces can be in three basic forms: restructuring (downsizing and cost reduction), reengineering (redesign of programs), and regenerating strategies (development of new competencies) (from Hamel and Prahalad, 1994). Of the three options, redesign and regeneration are by far the most attractive in terms of building organizational capacity. It is important to avoid the mind-set and perils of downsizing. If you must cut your budget, avoid doing less with less or more with less. Redesign or regeneration requires attention to the experiences, values, and current context of the organization as well as history. The authors emphasize that the future is not what will happen; it is what is happening now (Hamel and Prahalad, 1994). Most institutions have experience to draw on if they can identify and validate it.

Creating Clarity of Purpose. Before setting out on a journey, it is always wise to have a destination in mind as well as some idea about how to get there. That means you need both a vision and a sense of direction. It is not always easy to figure out who you are, who you want to be, and how you want to get there. The PSU experience revealed key questions that a campus community needs to ask itself (adapted from Hamel and Prahalad, 1994). These are truly scholarly questions and require different research methodologies to answer. Generally it is the role of the leader to ask these questions and insist on thoughtful, well-documented answers to key questions about our mission, our organizational values, the educational model we wanted to build, the resources we had to invest in our future, and the alliances we wanted to form.

Working in a Scholarly Mode at a Significant Scale. Intentional and significant change must be approached in a scholarly manner with the same demanding standards of excellence and the expectation that action will be guided by a warranted foundation. In other words, transformation must be guided by a well-documented and well-researched case. The approach to building such a case resembles the expectations that the scholarly community has for quality research in any field. The role of the academic leader in this model is identical to the principal investigator in any research project. The academic leader should be guided by the same standards that the scholarly community applies to the assessment of scholarly work. The only difference, and admittedly it is an important one, is that the result is not a scholarly communication but a transformed institution.

A particularly good source for insights on the standards that scholarship must meet is *Scholarship Assessed* (Glassick, Huber, and Maeroff, 1997). Using the Glassick model as a guide, the case for institutional change must have *clear goals* and must be firmly grounded in knowledge about the institution and the context in which it operates (*adequate preparation*). The warrant for change must be built on a solid body of evidence gathered and interpreted in a disciplined and principled way (*appropriate methods*) and shown to be significantly related to the challenges at hand (*significant results*). The case must be presented effectively (*effective presentation*) and studied reflectively (*reflective critique*), with a clear and compelling sense of responsibility for the effects of the ideas and proposed actions on the community that will be affected, both inside and outside the institution (*ethical and social responsibility*) (qualities in italics reflect Glassick, Huber, and Maeroff, 1997).

This list of standards leads to a more finely grained set of expectations for how an institution and its leadership can most effectively approach change at a transformational level. Change must be intentional and must affect a significant part of the institutional mission, for example, general education, undergraduate majors, research, and outreach. Change must be supported by a culture of evidence that documents the consequences of the steps undertaken and allows a community to learn from its experiences. When approaching institutional change, the nature of this community and the extent to which the process draws on the talents and expertise of individuals outside the academy as well as within the campus depend on the mission, history, and aspirations of the campus. Attention to the challenge of appropriate consultation can strengthen shared governance. Change, when approached as a scholarly act, must emerge from a consultative and scholarly process similar to the workings of a deliberative democracy. The development of a case for change and the choice of ways to create an academic community represent a form of public scholarship and will, for most institutions, include engagement with the broader community beyond the campus as well as an open and reflective process within the campus community (Brown, 2004).

Developing a Conducive Campus Environment. Leaders play a decisive role in helping campus employees to shift their mental models in order to engage in the change process. This section reviews some specific strategies used.

Starting Out Well. It is important to take care to pick the right first project and to be sure that it is both symbolic and substantive. Our goal was to debunk one of the major impediments to change: that an unidentified "they" would not allow us to do "it," whatever "it" was. Our choice of a project was illuminating, so to speak, for we chose to find out how many PSU employees it took to change a light bulb.

The campus lighting project met all of the conditions for a good first project. It would require us to study and learn the techniques of Total Quality Management in order to map out the steps in changing a light bulb from the time a bulb was reported to be out to the time that it was replaced so that we could learn where in the chain the process was broken or too complex and error prone. Success in the form of a well-lit campus would help us provide an existence proof to dispute the usual PSU explanation for why things could not change on campus ("THEY won't let us do that"). During periods of rapid change, a leader must surface the underlying mental models that can support resistance to change and hold them up to thoughtful scrutiny. This was a good project to start that process.

Making Connections and Sustaining Change. To be effective, the scope of change as it unfolds should include the major spheres central to the identity and purposes of the institution. For PSU, the four interlocking spheres were curricular reform, the definition of scholarship, collaboration with the community, and campus operations and management. So what did PSU do in order to bring these elements together? The list was daunting. During the first wave of reform, we redesigned our general education curriculum. We linked faculty roles to our institutional mission and purpose by redesigning our approach to promotion and tenure and by providing faculty-led support for professional development that would allow our faculty to interpret and introduce elements of engaged scholarship into their own research and their approach to the curriculum. We rethought how work is done at PSU and how to incorporate our own educational philosophy into the way we approached problem solving. We began to understand how important our students were in both contributing to our distinctive campus mission and connecting us to the surrounding community. They were members of that community themselves. We began to realign departmental priorities and values to reflect shared responsibilities and set up a meaningful link between the budget resource cycle and campus and unit priorities.

Fully aware that attention is paid to those things that are measured, we began to develop effective assessments of the educational experience of students and the impact of PSU on the community that reflected what we valued and wished to reward. The process of data gathering and interpretation allowed us to adopt a habit of reflective practice throughout the organization.

Only later did we discover that the name for this was a *learning organization* (the many definitions of a learning organization are outlined in Garvin, 1999). We also sought collaboration with other institutions within the Portland region and across the country. Through redesign of our curriculum and campus operations and through investments from private foundations, we began to identify and release sufficient resources to invest in change.

Rebalancing the Institution. By the time of our fiftieth anniversary in 1996, we were already partway through the second wave of change, and some of the elements of the next set of challenges beyond that were already fairly easy to see. The second wave of innovation and adaptation represented an impressive list of things that would need to be done to sustain change at such a grand scale. According to people at PSU (personal communication), some of these steps have been taken; others have yet to be realized. The list was a long one, each element of which was a natural consequence of what we did in the first wave of innovation. We began to think about how to expand our undergraduate curricular innovation to additional partner sites. We sought to connect the philosophy of our general education curriculum to the major and our overall concepts of liberal learning. We began to redesign our basic processes of budgeting, institutional studies, and assessment and planning to support informed decisions and further adjustments as we learned more.

Beyond that daunting set of recalibrations of PSU's basic internal structure and program design and its working relationships beyond its campus borders, additional questions were taking shape that would form the basis for yet a third wave of change. The elements of the third wave were not yet clear in 1996 but were still in the form of large, challenging questions. How were we going to pay for the start-up costs of our ambitious agenda? How would we assess the quality of the educational experiences we offered and find out what our students were actually learning? How might we draw the clear educational philosophy that underlies the general education curriculum into the rest of the curriculum? What does it really mean to be the hub of an educational network? Where would the support and the money come from to realize our vision for a university district surrounding and extending our campus that would be shared with the city and developed as a mixed-use environment?

None of these challenging questions had ready answers. All required further study, a habit of thoughtful inquiry, and a willingness to learn from the experience of the earlier stages of institutional transformation. To negotiate these difficult next-wave questions, PSU had to become a true learning community. As in the case of any other kind of education, institutional learning is never done.

Understanding Change Itself. The final step is to understand change itself and how to work effectively in an environment that has been unsettled by either external or internal uncertainties, or both, and that is not likely to settle down any time soon, if ever.

In retrospect, the PSU story is clear on this point even though it was not always so clear at the time. There are a few very important things that an institution must attend to if it wishes to move into a change mode and continue to identify and address the rippling outward of the consequences of transformational change. From the PSU experience, we can draw a few lessons, the PSU Principles, which may have general value for other institutions and other times.

First, it is important to have a clear mission and an action-oriented strategic plan that comes from the work of the campus community itself and its experiences. The plan must be built on a shared set of core organizational values and a sense of collective purpose. Second, it is rare for an institution to undertake a completely new direction. Generally there are already elements of that future present in the fabric of the institution and in the interests and activities of the campus community. It is important to identify aspects of the institution already aligned with promising future directions and develop a vocabulary to define and recognize these efforts.

Third, it is always helpful to call attention to work that supports and exemplifies the goals of the institution. This can be done by creating incentives, recognition, and rewards consistent with mission and goals and by ensuring early successes. In the complexity of daily life, many people fail to catch the significance of these early, often small successes. It is important for campus leadership to interpret them and celebrate them.

Fourth, it is important to link budget decisions and performance. Maria Montessori built an educational philosophy for children on the basis of guided choice and logical consequences. Campuses that wish to undertake significant and intentional change need to do the same. The most powerful way to do this is to maintain a scholarly discipline of gathering and interpreting the results of change and linking budget decisions to performance and strategic goals. In the process, it is important to give resistance respect; there is much to be learned from the objections of responsible critics. In the process of gathering information and responses from a broad constituency, campus leaders can demonstrate flexibility and invent as they go. Teaching people to accept and embrace the risk of not knowing how things will turn out is not easy. The actions of leadership must not send mixed signals about the importance of experimentation by declaring innovation to be a high value and then punishing anyone who tries something risky and fails at the attempt.

Finally, it is important for leadership to pay attention to how people are interpreting what is going on and to help promote organizational learning by explaining what the change means. Good leaders leave the essential work of change in the hands of faculty, staff, and students. They do not micromanage, but they do notice and repeat good stories that help everyone learn their role in the campus mission. At PSU, we often spoke of how faculty and staff would learn how to "map themselves" into the new institutional landscape (Ramaley, 2002). Leaders can help a campus move process along by encouraging informal networks and a sense of community and by trusting people to be intelligent, care about the organization, and do their best. Most of all, the leader can express pride in what the institution is learning and achieving.

Linking Educational Philosophy to Organizational Behavior

Armed with a compelling educational vision that draws on their own institutional history, mission, and conditions, leaders can evaluate institutional interventions or responses to conflicting external mandates or budget crises or societal pressures or social criticisms or demands from the governing board without losing their sense of purpose and direction. Strong attention to educational purposes can guide any institution, whatever its mission, through troubling times. Do these demands make educational sense? Will these changes help the institution achieve its educational goals? With an educational compass in hand, the institution and its leadership will be less likely to become distracted or drift off course. By using the lens of educational purpose and philosophy, a college or university can approach change in a scholarly way by defining and then following the dictates and expectations of a shared vision of what it means to exercise scholarly responsibility.

References

Brown, D. "What Is 'Public' About What Academics Do?" *Higher Education Exchange,* 2004, pp. 17–29.

Brown, J. S. "Growing Up Digital." *Change Magazine.* Mar.–Apr. 2000, pp. 11–20.

Dodds, G. *The College That Would Not Die: The First Fifty Years of Portland State University, 1946–1996.* Portland: Oregon Historical Society in collaboration with Portland State University, 2000.

Eckel, P., Green, M., and Hill, B. *On Change v. Riding the Waves of Change: Insights from Transforming Institutions.* Washington, D.C.: American Council on Education, 2001.

Gardner, H. *Leading Minds. An Anatomy of Leadership.* New York: Basic Books, 1995.

Garvin, D. A. *Learning in Action. A Guide to Putting the Learning Organization to Work.* Boston: Harvard Business School Press, 1999.

Glassick, C. E., Huber, M. T., and Maeroff, G. I. *Scholarship Assessed: Evaluation of the Professoriate.* San Francisco: Jossey-Bass, 1997.

Hamel, G., and Prahalad, C. K. *Competing for the Future.* Boston: Harvard Business School Press, 1994.

Heifetz, M. L. *Leading Change, Overcoming Chaos.* Berkeley, Calif.: Ten Speed Press, 1993.

House, E. R., and Howe, K. R. *Values in Evaluation and Social Research.* Thousand Oaks, Calif.: Sage, 1999.

Mark, M. M., Henry, G. T., and Julnes, G. *Evaluation: An Integrated Framework for Understanding, Guiding and Improving Policies and Programs.* San Francisco: Jossey-Bass, 2000.

Martin, R. R., Manning, K., and Ramaley, J. A. "The Self-Study as a Chariot for Strategic Change." In J. L. Ratcliff, E. S. Lubinescu, and M. A. Gaffney (eds.), *How Accreditation Influences Assessment.* New Directions for Higher Education, no. 113. San Francisco: Jossey-Bass, 2001.

Ramaley, J. A. "Large-Scale Institutional Change to Implement an Urban University Mission: Portland State University." *Journal of Urban Affairs,* 1996, *18*(2), 139–151.

Ramaley, J. A. "Change as a Scholarly Act: Higher Education Research Transfer to Practice." In A. Kezar and P. Eckel (eds.), *Moving Beyond the Gap Between Research and Practice in Higher Education.* New Directions for Higher Education, no. 110. San Francisco: Jossey-Bass, 2000.

Ramaley, J. A. "Moving Mountains: Institutional Culture and Transformational Change." In R. M. Diamond (ed.), *A Field Guide to Academic Leadership.* San Francisco: Jossey-Bass, 2002.

Russo, J. E., and Schoemaker, P. H. *Decision Traps.* New York: Simon and Schuster, 1989.

Senge, P. *The Fifth Discipline.* New York: Doubleday, 1990.

Wilson, J. Q. *Bureaucracy.* New York: Basic Books, 1989.

JUDITH A. RAMALEY *is Presidential Professor of Biomedical Sciences and a fellow of the Margaret Chase Smith Center at the University of Maine-Orono.*

BARBARA A. HOLLAND *is a senior scholar at Indiana University-Purdue University at Indianapolis and an adjunct professor at the University of Sydney.*

*The author articulates how she helped create learning
through a center for teaching and learning and other
strategies.*

Beyond Faculty Development: How Centers for Teaching and Learning Can Be Laboratories for Learning

Devorah Lieberman

Centers for teaching and learning have emerged across the country and around the globe in response to pedagogical needs in institutions of higher education. The original intent of these centers was to create a place on campus that focused on student learning and provided support to faculty in their efforts to meet student learning (Tiberius, 2002). Often doctoral-granting institutions graduated new doctoral students with deep knowledge of their discipline and research methodologies. However, those who intended to continue within the professoriate were often underprepared in appropriate pedagogical theory and practice. These faculty had earned their terminal degrees within a discipline, learned how to conduct research, and then when hired in tenure-track positions discovered that although they had a background in the discipline, they lacked a foundation in the best pedagogical practices (Kalivoda, Broder, and Jackson, 2003). Centers for teaching and learning were providing the faculty with the pedagogical theory and practice that they needed to teach at both the graduate and undergraduate levels.

Concurrent with the growth of these centers has been a dramatic shift from a focus on teaching to a focus on student learning and social constructivism (Lieberman and Guskin, 2003). This shift draws attention to learning as a "process of enculturation into a community of practice by means of social interaction among learners and between learners and teachers" (Tiberius, 2002, p. 30). Centers for teaching and learning recognized this shift from a focus on teaching to a focus on student learning and assisted the faculty as well with this change in perspective. This meant that these centers addressed which teaching and learning strategies would most assist the students in a particular learning environment rather than focusing primarily on what tools the professor should employ. During these formative years, centers for teaching and learning focused on a mixture of the following goals: (1) developing the teacher-student relationship as a vehicle for learning, (2) assisting teachers with content mastery, (3) assisting teachers with style and delivery, and (4) helping teachers become facilitators of learning (Tiberius, 2002).

In the early 1990s, when higher education began to seriously examine the relationship among curricula, student retention, and student learning outcomes, conditions were ripe for deep organizational learning that would lead to organizational change (Eckel, Green, and Hill, 2001). As Kezar noted in Chapter One in this volume, in retrospect it would have been valuable to examine how institutions approached their organizational learning and what conditions existed within their organizations (see Chapter One). The American Council on Education was one organization that recognized the need to systematically study this process (Eckel, 2002).

During this same period in higher education, in order to meet these changing needs within institutions, many centers for teaching and learning began shifting from a focus on only teaching and learning strategies to becoming the broader institutional laboratories necessary for a learning organization. Yet other centers were created to include both support for teaching and learning as well as organizational learning. Traditional centers for teaching and learning began to see themselves more holistically, serving the institution in ways much broader than providing teaching tools and student learning tools. These centers began organizing for learning and sought to assess institutional efforts to link student learning with the mission of the institution in relation to curriculum, pedagogy, and method of delivery; faculty recruitment; developing scholarship in support of improved teaching and learning; rewards and incentives; organizational structures and processes; information resources and planning capacity; and student services and cocurricular activities and resources and facilities. These centers assisted their institutions in becoming learning organizations by focusing on "the degree to which the institution had developed the systems to assess its own performance and to use information to improve student learning over time that was systematic and regular, reinforced a climate of inquiry throughout the institution, reflected their influx of stakeholders and an awareness of the distinctive characteristics of its own students; identified key dimensions of performance that included student learning, and was based on standards of evidence that prominently featured educational results" (Western Association of Schools and Colleges, 2001, pp. 6–7).

These centers supported the learning organization process and became the institutions' laboratories for learning as well as springboards to assist change across the campuses. Activities that encouraged organizational learning became critical components of the centers. These activities tended to include, but were not limited to, moving the institution toward (1) decentralization, (2) increased trust between administration and faculty, (3) enhanced communication among campus constituents, (4) greater information flow throughout campus constituents, and (5) faculty and staff development and training of newly introduced concepts and procedures (Kezar, Chapter One).

Portland State University (PSU) in Portland, Oregon, and Wagner College on Staten Island, New York, are examples of two institutions that share characteristics considered common to high-functioning learning organizations. Each has organized for learning through different paths, yet each has instituted processes that created environments that encourage faculty to be at the front as well as at the center of their institution's organizational learning. The following descriptions of PSU and Wagner College highlight the factors that were critical for creating and sustaining their respective laboratories for organizational learning within their institutional learning organizations.

The learning organization analyses proffered about PSU and about Wagner College stem from personal experience as well as a thorough review of the organizational learning and learning organization literature. The PSU analysis is grounded in the sixteen and one-half years of experience at the institution where I held positions as a faculty member, department chair, director of teaching and learning, and vice provost and special assistant to the president.

Beyond Faculty Development: Key Elements Across Learning Organizations

Initiating a proactive approach to organizational learning and striving to be learning organizations, PSU and Wagner College both create and further individual and group interactions that shape their respective organizational systems. Both strive to create processes for acquiring information, interpreting the data acquired, developing new knowledge, and sustaining this learning as they approach systemwide change.

Moving from one learning organization (PSU) to another learning organization (Wagner College), both of which approach their organizational learning through different organizational structures, the following highlight eight common elements that exist across both:

- Maintain a scholarly approach to answering institutionwide research questions.
- Approach the campus-based research questions as learners rather than experts.
- Develop an iterative culture of evidence.

- Recognize and reward the institution and its participants for functioning as a learning organization.
- Link organizational learning to the institutional mission.
- Assist faculty in developing strong connections with each other and the institution rather than viewing their discipline as their only affinity group.
- Have faith in the learning organization.
- There is no one size fits all organizational learning model.

Spotlighting Organizational Learning at Portland State University

In the 1990s, the administrative leadership at PSU intentionally positioned the institution to be a learning organization. Their goal was to include individuals, groups, and the institution at large in major institutional change, beginning with the complete redesign of its undergraduate general education, integrating civic engagement into the mission statement and also weaving it throughout the curriculum, and rethinking promotion and tenure guidelines so that they reflected the changes in institutional values and expectations. These changes were grounded in the following principles:

- The administration and the faculty would work together collaboratively toward a common goal.
- Institutional change would be based on learning from within the institution as well as learning from other institutions.
- Faculty, administrators, and students would actively participate in "telling the Portland State University" story at conferences and in publications.

In January 1995, the Center for Academic Excellence (CAE) was created, through faculty and administration collaboration, to serve as the laboratory for organizational learning and to further PSU as a learning organization. Three areas central in the institutional mission became the focus of the CAE: teaching and learning, civic engagement, and assessment. If there were to be dramatic institutional changes, then PSU as a learning organization needed to have a place on the campus that could assist with organizational learning. This place became the CAE.

Aligned with Garvin's approach to learning organizations (2000), the CAE constructed itself as a campus laboratory addressing systematic problem solving, experimentation with new approaches, learning from experience and past history, learning from experience and best practices of others, and transferring knowledge efficiently. When the CAE was established, the PSU president and the provost announced that the CAE and the university would be an institution that had two organizing principals: it would take a scholarly approach to change, and all institutional change processes would be grounded in a culture of evidence. A fundamental goal of the CAE was to support an environment that promotes a culture of learning, a community of learners, and that individual learning enriches and enhances the organization as a whole.

Spotlighting Organizational Learning at Wagner College

Much like PSU, Wagner College administrators and faculty together designed and implemented an undergraduate education program that united the faculty, was aligned with the institutional mission, connected liberal arts and professional programs, introduced systematic reflective practice and civic engagement, and increased student retention between freshman and sophomore years.

The faculty and administration in 1998 implemented the Wagner Plan, a newly designed general education program. All students entering and graduating from Wagner College participate in the Wagner Plan throughout each of their college years. This novel approach to student learning emphasizes both traditionally structured modes of learning and experiential learning (field-based learning, or learning by doing). Students participate in at least three learning communities, of which two include field work, research, or an internship in an organization, usually in New York City or the surrounding area. The first-year learning community includes a field-based experience that is thematically linked to two introductory liberal arts courses and a reflective tutorial, in which students reflect on and write about the content of their courses and its relationship to their community experiences. The second- and third-year learning communities consist of two thematically linked disciplinary courses that serve as an important bridge between the first- and fourth-year learning communities. The fourth-year learning community, which is in the student's major, consists of a capstone course in the discipline, a substantial internship or research experience, and a major paper or presentation in the senior reflective tutorial. The three learning communities individually and collectively challenge students to relate academic learning to the wider world, social issues, and their own individual experiences.

Wagner College is a learning organization without having a specified center to serve as the laboratory for organizational learning; rather, it has strategically created opportunities for organizational learning in separate pockets of the campus.

Implementing the Key Elements of Learning

This section outlines the key features that leaders can use to fashion an environment that is conducive to learning. I will review the efforts of two different institutions to create organizational learning among faculty. The approaches they take are quite different, but the results are similar.

Maintain a Scholarly Approach to Answering Institutionwide Research Questions

Portland State University. In order to keep activities and mission in the context of a learning organization, the CAE took a scholarly approach to answering questions of concern to the institution. These questions were usually stated in the form of research-type questions or hypotheses. The questions were then followed by a review of literature, a pilot test or project, an analysis, and then a strategic plan for integration. For example, in 1991, the president and provost appointed a group of carefully selected and volunteer faculty and administrators who asked, "Why is our freshman-to-sophomore retention rate so low?" In order to take a scholarly approach to answering this question, this group examined the existing data; reviewed the national literature on student retention; collected data by interviewing faculty, staff, and current students and conducting focus groups; created a campus document with the results of their investigation; held campuswide colloquia sharing their findings; made recommendations for a pilot program at PSU based on their findings, the literature, and activities on other campuses; implemented and assessed the pilot; implemented a new general education program based on the pilot program assessment; and built in ongoing assessment of the general education program.

Wagner College. Intending to design a successful student-centered undergraduate education program, the faculty in the college consciously pursued this goal using a scholarly approach. In order to do this, they embraced and practiced the elements of a learning organization: (1) believe that the efforts and power of the group lie with groups of faculty, not solely with the administration; (2) support trust between administration and faculty; (3) engage in further communication among campus constituents; (4) enhance information flow throughout campus constituents; and (5) train faculty and staff in newly introduced concepts and procedures. Concurrent with these elements, they researched which and why general education programs were effective in other institutions. They analyzed these practices and used the information to build the Wagner Plan, which addressed their student population's particular needs in the light of the unique factor of existing within the New York metropolitan region.

Approach the Campus-Based Research Questions as Learners Rather Than Experts

Portland State University. The assumption that faculty are the experts and students the learners is status quo in traditional institutions of higher education. The work of faculty in institutions is routine and modeled after their faculty mentors dating back to their life in graduate school. In learning organizations, faculty are learners as well. Faculty expect students to go through a learning process as they acquire and apply information in their course work. Similarly, faculty as learners in the learning organization go through learning stages as well: acquiring information, interpreting information, and applying information (Garvin, 2000).

Viewing faculty as learners in the learning organization was an important component of PSU. Historically, faculty were perceived as experts and students as learners. In the PSU learning organization, faculty were not considered experts and participated in the process in ways that they were learning about the organization, the change process, and their role in the process of institutional change (R. Guarasci, personal communication, Sept. 10, 2004).

Wagner College. Once the Wagner Plan was created and implemented, it was critical that organizational learning continue in relation to student learning, the Wagner Plan, and other campus and community constituents within the system. In order to ensure that the concept of all faculty learning and growing together continued, faculty and administrators jointly selected coordinators for the First Year Program, Intermediate Learning Communities, and the Senior Year Program. These positions report to the dean of learning communities. The coordinators are entrusted with responsibilities that sustain faculty and administrator trust, decentralize policy development, maintain open communication and information flow with those who participate in the Wagner Plan and those who are peripheral to the plan, and structure faculty development sessions that focus on teaching and learning within the Wagner Plan context.

Wagner faculty continue to select these coordinators from among their own ranks. The scholarly approach to continue ongoing assessment reinforces the concept that no faculty are the experts in the college's organizational learning; rather, all faculty participating in the Wagner Plan are learning from the process and from each other.

Develop an Iterative Culture of Evidence

Portland State University. The PSU administration began using the phrase "culture of evidence" in the mid-1990s. As a learning organization, it was imperative that faculty, staff, and students assumed that the PSU way of doing business was evidence based. The PSU president, Judith Ramaley (1990–1996), understood at the early stages of the undergraduate general education reform that the culture of evidence would become the standard for addressing types of learning within the institution: intelligence, experience, and experimentation (Garvin, 2000).

In 1999, when the Commission on Campus Climate and Life recommended that assessment become one of the ongoing campuswide initiatives, it became apparent that the faculty as learners within the organization recognized that the culture of evidence and assessment was a critical element of organizational learning. Traditionally, faculty might ask when an initiative relinquishes the name *initiative* and becomes part of the institutional fabric. In a learning organization, this may never happen because initiatives are continually assessed and reassessed in order for organizational learning to occur. Although an initiative may become institutionalized, the ongoing assessment is important. Each year, many PSU faculty would ask if the campuswide initiatives had been achieved, assuming that institutional success was measured by the achievement and thus closure of an initiative. President Dan Bernstine reinforced that these initiatives could be measured quantitatively, but that as organizational learning occurred through ongoing assessment, they were still very much a part of PSU, a learning organization.

Wagner College. As a new administrator in a leadership position at Wagner College, entering an institution that is becoming a learning organization, the provost's responsibilities link to furthering the college in its organizational learning as it becomes a more efficient and more effective learning organization. Although a specific office recognized by the campus system as the laboratory for organizational learning does not exist at Wagner, the campus is creating a culture that approaches research questions in relation to the institution in a scholarly manner with faculty as learners and evidence-based assessment as fundamental to organizational learning. It is important to recognize that the shift from traditional organizations to learning organizations often occurs when the campus can coalesce around a change issue that affects the campus deeply and broadly. Faculty development and assessment during this process relate to supporting faculty to think differently about their roles and approaches when they are in a learning organization.

In the absence of a teaching and learning center or a center for academic excellence, an organizational structure exists at Wagner College that helps serve as a campus laboratory. This structure, through learning community coordinators (first year coordinator, institutional learning center [ILC] coordinator, senior learning community coordinator, dean of learning communities), provides ongoing consistent organizational learning in efforts to maintain a healthy learning organization. As an institution committed to creating a positive student learning environment, the Wagner faculty understand the importance of ongoing data collection, performed in ways that provide ongoing evaluation and assessment. In lieu of a center or laboratory, an existing committee framework seeks to continually collect data and suggest changes to curriculum, organizational design, and future developments.

Undergirding all of these committee structures and policy recommending procedures is the assumption that Wagner's continual improvement is accomplished through an iterative process resulting in greater student learning.

Recognize and Reward the Institution and Its Participants for Functioning as a Learning Organization

Portland State University. During the process of implementing the PSU Undergraduate Education Program and CAE, the faculty and administrators created new and aligned promotion and tenure guidelines. Consequently, the presentation and publications of faculty who research PSU as a learning organization are recognized as scholarship for purposes of promotion and tenure.

Wagner College. Service to the institution is seriously considered within the promotion, tenure, and reappointment process at Wagner College. Consequently, faculty who actively participate in aspects of Wagner's organizational learning are recognized within personnel decision making. Examples of where organizational learning and service are highly rewarded in this process are seen in serving on and actively participating in the Committee on Learning Assessment, the Academic Personnel Committee, the Faculty Personnel Committee, or the Priorities and Budget Committee or serving as a coordinator of one of the three learning communities in the Wagner Plan: the First Year Program, the Intermediate Learning Community, or the Senior Learning Community.

Link Organizational Learning to the Institutional Mission

Portland State University. The institutional mission is the constant as the organizational learning process unfolds (Kezar, 2001). The ongoing and consistent assessment of the learning that occurs within the institution is measured against its articulated mission. The PSU mission is to enhance the intellectual, social, cultural, and economic qualities of urban life by providing access throughout the life span to a quality liberal education for undergraduates and an appropriate array of professional and graduate programs especially relevant to metropolitan areas.

To this end, PSU has the following goals:

• A high-quality educational environment
• Creation of knowledge
• Local, regional, national, and global impact
• The urban laboratory
• Meeting the needs of contemporary society
• Meeting the needs of a diverse community

The mission of the CAE was grounded in socially constructing campus views of scholarship, civic engagement, the shift from teachers to learners, and a focus on student learning. By 1999, the formal charge of the CAE was to integrate, assess, and continually improve the following throughout the university:

• Civic engagement
• Assessment
• Technology
• Best pedagogical practices
• Best student advising practices
• Diversity
• Internationalization

Wagner College. Wagner, as a high-functioning learning organization, seeks to ground organizational learning in its institutional mission: "Wagner

College prepares students for life, as well as for careers, by emphasizing scholarship, achievement, leadership, and citizenship. Wagner offers a comprehensive educational program that is anchored in the liberal arts, experiential and co-curricular learning, interculturalism, interdisciplinary studies, and service to society and that is cultivated by a faculty dedicated to promoting individual expression, reflective practice, and integrative learning" (Wagner College, 2005).

The elected, appointed, and volunteer committee and cohort structures at Wagner College are structured and organized in such a way that they directly carry out and support the mission of the institution. Consequently, all organizational learning is also aligned with the institutional mission.

Assist Faculty in Developing Strong Connections with Each Other and the Institution Rather Than Viewing Their Discipline as Their Only Affinity Group. Two other factors that contribute to an institution's becoming a high-functioning learning organization are faculty perceptions that they are no longer individuals but that they are integral parts of the greater whole of the institution and faculty commitment to the institution as a high priority. Traditionally, faculty have viewed themselves as individuals within the organization, not necessarily seeing their connection with or relationship to other faculty throughout the institutions. Second, many faculty feel a commitment to a discipline and less so to a particular educational institution. When faculty, staff, and students view themselves within a more holistic system and see the significance of their place within the institution, they develop a greater affinity with their colleagues and their institution. There is then a greater likelihood that they will hold deep beliefs about their commitment to the institution as a learning organization.

Portland State University. The CAE provided the opportunity for faculty to be committed to the institution and to their colleagues and together to assume the learner roles in each of the institutional initiatives. An example occurred in 1999 when a group of faculty and staff were appointed by PSU President Bernstine as members of the PSU Commission on Campus Climate and Life. In following a scholarly approach to answer the question, "What needs to occur at PSU in order for it to be a campus that creates a culture of quality?" the commission assumed a scholarly approach and viewed themselves as learners in this process. The commission's final report to President Bernstine resulted in four recommendations and initiatives: (1) thread diversity through the faculty, staff, students, and curricula; (2) create a student-centered advising system; (3) internationalize the faculty, staff, and curricula; and (4) implement a faculty-designed and faculty-driven ongoing assessment process throughout the institution that leads to improved student learning.

Wagner College. Wagner College fosters both strong support for disciplinary commitment and institutional affinity. This is accomplished when new faculty join Wagner College faculty ranks. All new tenure-track faculty teach within the First Year Program. Immediately they join an affinity group outside their discipline. They have a three-year commitment to the First Year Program, which means that they will teach with another faculty member from a different department for three years, participate in multiple First Year Program meetings that focus on Wagner and general education issues, and attend a First Year Program spring retreat. Other examples of dual commitment to the institution and the respective disciplines can be seen through Wagner's interdisciplinary mentor-mentee program, interdisciplinary faculty forums, interdisciplinary committee structures, strategic and ongoing campus-based social activities, honors and awards for scholarship, teaching, and service.

Have Faith in the Learning Organization. Both PSU and Wagner attract and retain faculty who are afforded the opportunity to question the institution's processes and its goals. This is part of the beauty and charm of a learning organization. Both PSU and Wagner, as high-functioning learning organizations, have created systems and processes that encourage faculty, staff, students, and administrators to step forward and participate in the organizational learning process in ways that enhance the institution. What may be perceived as resistance by some becomes part of the learning process when it is embraced by the organizational learning structure. It is institutions like these that should be most recognized and applauded as learning organizations.

There Is No One Size Fits All Organizational Learning Model: Beyond Faculty Development

Portland State University. Within a few years, the CAE became the nexus and laboratory for organizational learning at PSU. When a question was asked about the role of PSU in relation to the mission statement and goals, CAE became the natural laboratory for faculty, staff, and administrators to approach the question in a scholarly manner, as learners, and with ongoing consistent assessment.

Wagner College. The standing committees and the organizational structure supporting ongoing data collection and continual improvement serve as Wagner College's overarching institutional laboratory. Evidence of the college's existence as a learning organizations is the continuing evolution of the 1996 creation of the Wagner Plan with the goal of ongoing improvement of student learning, enhancing community-based learning and civic engagement, increasing reflective practice, and bridging the liberal arts and professional programs.

Conclusion

Developing faculty to survive and thrive within the learning organization is part of today's institutions of higher education. Faculty development in these institutions focuses on assisting faculty with their shift from expert to learner, from having the answers to seeking answers to campus based research questions, from working independently to working collaboratively, and from perceiving the institution as their affinity group along with their academic discipline. Successful higher education learning organizations are those that support these forms of organizational learning, whether in a laboratory faculty development center or integrated throughout the institutional structure.

References

Eckel, P. "Institutional Transformation and Change: Insights for Faculty Developers. *To Improve the Academy,* 20, pp. 3–17. Bolton, Mass.: Anker, 2002.

Eckel, P., Green, M., and Hill, B. *Riding the Waves of Change: Insights for Transforming Institutions.* Washington, D.C.: American Council on Education, 2001.

Garvin, D. *Learning in Action: A Guide to Putting the Learning Organization to Work.* Boston: Harvard Business School Press, 2000.

Kalivoda, P., Broder, J., and Jackson, W. "Establishing a Teaching Academy: Cultivation of Teaching at a Research University Campus." *To Improve the Academy,* 21, pp.79–92. Bolton, Mass.: Anker, 2003.

Kezar, A. *Understanding and Facilitating Organizational Change in the Twenty-First Century: Recent Research and Conceptualizations.* Washington, D.C.: ASHE-ERIC, 2001.

Lieberman, D., and Guskin, D. "The Essential Role of Faculty Development in New Higher Education Models." *To Improve the Academy,* 21, pp. 257–272. Bolton, Mass.: Anker, 2003.

Tiberius, R. "A Brief History of Educational Development: Implications for Teachers and Developers." *To Improve the Academy,* 20, pp. 20–38. Bolton, Mass.: Anker Press, 2002.

Wagner College. "Wagner Mission Statement and Wagner Plan Description." 2005. http://www.wagner.edu/presmess/mission.html.

Western Association of Schools and Colleges. *WASC Handbook of Accreditation.* Alameda, Calif.: Western Association of Schools and Colleges, 2001.

DEVORAH LIEBERMAN is the provost and vice president for academic affairs at Wagner College on Staten Island, New York.

8

The author uses the theory and process of organizational learning to make a case for how to understand and address the cultural and structural barriers that preclude colleges and universities from producing equitable educational outcomes for students.

Closing the Achievement Gap in Higher Education: An Organizational Learning Perspective

Estela Mara Bensimon

In this chapter I address one of the most urgent and intractable problems in higher education—inequality in educational outcomes for historically under-served groups—from the perspective of organizational learning theory. Historically, in the higher education research community, the study of minority students has been primarily through the lens of student development theories. (In this chapter, I use the terms *minority* and *underrepresented* interchangeably to refer to racial and ethnic groups that are experiencing the greatest achievement gaps as measured by traditional educational indicators such as attainment of the bachelor's degree: Puerto Ricans, Mexican Americans, African Americans, Native Americans, Native Hawaiians, and others.) I propose that the theory and processes of organizational learning can help researchers and practitioners understand and address the structural and cultural obstacles that prevent colleges and universities from producing equitable educational outcomes. Organization learning, in both theory and practice, is particularly effective in making the invisible visible and the undiscussable discussable, two conditions that aptly describe the status of race- and ethnic-based unequal outcomes on most campuses.

Among the many factors that contribute to the invisibility of unequal college outcomes for underrepresented minorities, an obvious one is that

The study on which this chapter is based, "Designing and Implementing a Diversity Scorecard to Improve Institutional Effectiveness for Underserved Minority Students," is funded by the James Irvine Foundation. The findings and opinions here are solely those of the author and do not reflect the position or priorities of the foundation.— Bensimon the disaggregation of student outcome data by race and ethnicity (and by gender within racial and ethnic categories) is not an institutionalized practice. Institutional practices develop from and reflect the shared cognitive frames of institutional participants. Cognitive frames, also known as mental maps, represent "the rules or reasoning" that govern how individuals interpret situations and how they design and implement their actions (Argyris, 1991). Organizational learning theory can help us understand the nature of cognitive frames and the ways in which some reveal patterns of unequal outcomes, while others hide them. If patterns of inequality are invisible, they will not be discussed, and if institutional participants do not have a reason or opportunity to talk about unequal outcomes, the problem will not be addressed directly.

I am concerned here with a particular kind of organizational learning problem: the persistence of unequal educational outcomes for racial and ethnic groups with a history of past discrimination in postsecondary education. I view inequality in educational outcomes as a learning problem of institutional actors—faculty members, administrators, counselors, and others—rather than as a learning problem of students, the more typical interpretation (Garmoran and others, 2003). The problem of unequal outcomes resides within individuals, in the cognitive frames that govern their attitudes, beliefs, values, and actions. Similarly, the reduction of inequalities also lies within individuals, specifically, in their capacity to develop equity as their cognitive frame. That is, individuals whose institutional roles can influence whether students are successful or not need to learn cognitive processes that enable them to think about the situation of underrepresented students and their outcomes through the lens of equity. To put it simply, faculty members, counselors, and institutional leaders need to become equity minded. However, even if they were to consider the educational status of underrepresented students within their own institutions or departments (reflection on the educational outcomes of minorities is not a routine practice in most institutions of higher education), institutional actors are more predisposed to do so from the standpoint of diversity or deficit. Institutional actors are more likely to view diversity as a generalized characteristic of institutions and be blind to the particular circumstances of the racial and ethnic groups that constitute diversity. Or if they are or become aware of the educational status of specific racial/ethnic groups within their own campuses and departments, they are more likely to make stereotypical attributions, such as associating deficit with blacks and Hispanics and achievement with whites and Asians.

The Role of Individuals in Organizational Learning

The key concepts in regard to individuals are that (1) learning is done by individuals who are members of an organizational entity such as a college or university, an administrative division, an academic department, or a research team; (2) individuals inquire into a problem collectively, on behalf of an organizational entity (Huber, 1991); and (3) organizational culture and structures can promote or inhibit individual learning (Argyris and Schön, 1996; Kezar, Glenn, Lester, and Nakamoto, 2004).

Contrary to the dominant belief that the solution to unequal educational outcomes lies in a new program or technique, somewhere out there, that has been validated as a "best practice," I (along with my colleagues at the Center for Urban Education) believe that institutional actors, as a consequence of their beliefs, expectations, values, and practices, create or perpetuate unequal outcomes and that the possibility for reversing inequalities depends on individual learning that holds the potential for bringing about self-change. That is, individuals—the ways in which they teach, think students learn, and connect with students, and the assumptions they make about students based on their race or ethnicity—can create the problem of unequal outcomes. Such individuals, if placed in situations where they learn the ways in which their own thinking creates or accentuates inequities, can also learn new ways of thinking that are more equity minded. Individually and collectively, campus members can be the creators of the conditions that result in unequal or equitable outcomes.

What Is a Cognitive Frame? I use the concept of cognitive frame to describe the interpretive frameworks through which individuals make sense of phenomena. A cognitive frame is the way in which an individual understands a situation. Cognitive frames represent conceptual maps and determine what questions may be asked, what information is collected, how problems are defined, and what action should be taken (Bensimon, 1989; Bensimon and Neumann, 1993; Neumann, 1989; Neumann and Bensimon, 1990). Understanding cognitive frames is important because at the same time that frames make some things visible, they also function as cognitive blinders in that whatever is out of frame may be imperceptible (Bensimon, 1990).

Over time, individuals develop cognitive frames that represent implicit sense-making theories to help them interpret why things are as they are. Cognitive frames are reflections of how individuals think; they represent the cognitive "rules or reasoning" they use to design and implement their actions" (Argyris, 1991). Cognitive frames are important because they help us understand the ways in which individuals can manufacture inequality, as well as reduce it.

The Cognitive Frames of Diversity, Deficit, and Equity. Briefly, when individuals are guided by diversity as their cognitive frame (see Bensimon, Hao, and Bustillos, forthcoming, for a more expanded discussion of the three cognitive frames), they focus their attention on demographic characteristics of the student body, and view diversity in terms of interracial contact and human relations. Diversity is also viewed as an institutional characteristic that promotes learning outcomes and better prepares students for an increasingly diverse workforce and society. For example, the Supreme Court's ruling in favor of the University of Michigan's consideration of race as a criterion for admission to the law school is based on the premise that universities have a "compelling interest in attaining a diverse student body" because diversity yields educational benefits, promotes cross-racial understanding, and so forth (*Grutter v. Bollinger,* 2003).

Individuals with a deficit cognitive frame may value diversity and have positive attitudes toward increasing minority student participation in higher education, but they are inclined to attribute differences in educational outcomes for black, Hispanic, and Native American students, such as lower rates of retention or degree completion, to cultural stereotypes, inadequate socialization, or lack of motivation and initiative on the part of the students. The deficit cognitive frame is expressed in disapproving attributions such as complaining that "minority students" do not take advantage of the tutorial and academic support services the institution makes available. It can also be conveyed in well-meaning but pessimistic attributions, such as concluding that students cannot be expected to overcome the disadvantages of poverty and underpreparation; therefore, unequal outcomes are to be expected. Attributions framed by a deficit perspective imply that the academic difficulties of minority students are either self-inflicted or a natural outcome of socioeconomic and educational background. Essentially, from a deficit perspective, unequal outcomes are a problem without a solution.

Diversity-minded individuals are attuned to demographic differences; for example, they will comment on how diverse the student population is or how it lacks diversity, but more likely than not, they will be blind to the fact that the very students whose presence makes campus diversity possible are themselves experiencing unequal educational outcomes. In contrast, individuals whose beliefs and actions are guided by the deficit cognitive frame may be cognizant that their student body is diverse, and they may also be cognizant that there are racial disparities in educational outcomes, but they are impervious to the fact that they attribute the problem to the students and fail to take into account their own roles in the creation or solution of unequal outcomes. In sum, diversity-minded individuals may embrace diversity but not take into account racial achievement patterns (Pollock, 2001), and deficit-minded individuals take note of racial achievement patterns but treat them as "natural" in the light of the individuals' cultural, socioeconomic, and educational backgrounds.

Individuals who are guided by the equity cognitive frame focus intentionally on the educational results or outcomes of black, Hispanic, and Native American students. They are color conscious in an affirmative sense. For example, they are more prone to notice and question patterns of educational outcomes, and they are also more likely to view inequalities in the context of a history of exclusion, discrimination, and educational apartheid. Most important, equity-minded individuals are far more likely to understand that the beliefs, expectations, and actions of individuals influence whether minority group students are construed as being capable or incapable. Table 8.1 compares the three cognitive frames on four dimensions: orientation, discourse, strategy, and guiding questions.

Table 8.1. Diversity, Deficit, and Equity Cognitive Frames Compared on Four Dimensions

	Diversity Cognitive Frame	Deficit Cognitive Frame	Equity Cognitive Frame
Orientation	Focus on the representation of differences (for example, gender, race, ethnicity, sexual orientation, religion, and so on) in the student body	Focus on stereotypical characteristics associated with the culture of disadvantage and poverty	Focus on institutional practices and the production of unequal educational outcomes for minority group students
Discourse	Celebrating diversity, crossracial relationships, and color-blindness, enhancing access, cognitive and social benefits of having a diverse student body	Lack of preparation, motivation, study skills, blaming students and/or their backgrounds	Institutional responsibility for student outcomes, the manifestation of institutionalized racism, color-conscious, awareness of racialized practices and their differential consequences, awareness of white privilege
Strategies	Workshops, sensitivity training, exposing whites to the "other," diversifying the curriculum, creating inter-cultural centers	Compensatory educational programs, remedial courses, special programs, all focused on fixing the student	Changing institutions, developing institutional accountability of equitable educational outcomes, changing individuals' cognitive frames

In most institutions of higher education, the discourses of deficit and diversity are more likely to be heard than the discourse of equity. But the kinds of personal and institutional changes needed to eliminate the achievement gap are more likely to originate from equity thinking, which raises the following questions: In what ways can equity thinking be encouraged? In what ways might we shift individuals' cognitive frames from deficit and diversity toward equity? More to the point, what kinds of structures and processes might produce individual and collective learning that brings about equity thinking? In the section that follows, I offer ways of considering these questions, but with a caveat. Given the intractability of the problem of racial inequity in the United States, it would be foolhardy to claim a solution. Instead, what I offer is a way of thinking about the problem, one that is grounded in the theory of organization learning.

Equity Thinking Requires Double-Loop Learning. Argyris and Schön (1996) differentiate between two types of learning: single loop and double loop. Single-loop learners are prone to externalize problems by attributing them to forces and circumstances that are beyond their control and to resort to compensatory strategies as the treatment for problems that are perceived as dysfunctions. In single-loop learning, the focus is on reestablishing stability and normality by enacting corrections and eliminating errors. Solutions that come from single-loop learning focus on the external manifestations of the problem and leave internal values, norms, and beliefs intact—hence, the label *single loop.*

For example, individuals who have a deficit cognitive frame turn the focus of unequal outcomes away from their own attitudes, beliefs, and behaviors to those of the students. They externalize the problem and by so doing bring their "own learning to a grinding halt" (Argyris, 1991, p. 7). To put it simply, they fail to see how changes in their own attitudes, beliefs, and practices could reverse unequal outcomes.

Double-loop learning focuses attention on the root causes of a problem and the changes that need to be made in the attitudes, values, beliefs, and practices of individuals to bring about enduring results (Bauman, 2002). Looking inward is the capacity to reflect on how practices (also beliefs and expectations) at the individual and institutional levels produce racial inequalities. In particular, according to Argyris (1991), individuals "must learn how the very way they go about defining and solving problems can be a source of the problems in its own right" (p. 2).

Simply put, the difference between single-loop and double-loop learning is that in the former, change is at a surface level, whereas in the latter, the change is in underlying norms, beliefs, and principles (Coburn, 2003). Thus, bringing about a cognitive shift from diversity to equity or from deficit to equity involves double-loop learning.

The development of equity as a cognitive frame is a double-loop learning problem because it requires the willingness of individuals (1) to make the disaggregating of data on student outcomes by race/ethnicity and gender a routine and necessary practice to self-assess progress toward equity in educational outcomes; (2) identify equity in educational outcomes as an essential indicator of institutional performance and quality; and (3) assume responsibility for the elimination of unequal results.

Inquiry as a Method of Developing New Cognitive Frames

Bringing about a cognitive shift in individuals whose dominant frames are diversity or deficit requires an approach that enables them to see, on their own and as concretely as possible, racial and ethnic patterns in educational outcomes. Over the past three years, researchers at the University of Southern California's Center for Urban Education have been experimenting with such an approach. This approach, which is described in detail in other publications (Bensimon, 2004; Bensimon, Polkinghorne, Bauman, and Vallejo, 2004; www.usc.edu/dept/education/CUE), is designed to create or intensify awareness of equity or inequity by organizing campus members, such as professors, counselors, and deans, into inquiry teams that have been dubbed *evidence teams* because their role is to collect data on student outcomes disaggregated by race and ethnicity and analyze them. Their purpose is to hold a mirror up to their institution that reflects clearly and unambiguously the status of underrepresented students with respect to basic educational outcomes. Through inquiry, it is expected that individuals will learn of the nature of racial patterns in educational outcomes. By "learning," I mean noticing and seeing—that is, developing an awareness that racial and ethnic patterns of inequalities exist. By "equity," I mean that the outcomes of minority group students should more closely reflect their representation in the student body (for a more technical definition, see Bensimon, Hao, and Bustillos, forthcoming). Some individuals lack complete awareness, while others have a generalized sense of them; thus, for some individuals, there is a need to develop initial awareness, and for others there is a need to intensify their awareness. The challenge is how to develop or intensify equity-oriented awareness.

The critical importance of learning new or intensified awareness is exemplified by some of the initial reactions of individuals who were appointed by their presidents to serve on campus evidence teams. For example, a dean whose president had appointed him as the leader of the campus's evidence team told us on our first meeting, "We are 100 percent diverse. The Equity Scorecard may be relevant for other institutions like yours [meaning the University of Southern California], but we don't need to do that [disaggregate]; we know what it will look like . . . for us there are no differences by ethnicity." Clearly, this individual was aware of diversity as an institutional characteristic and could not entertain the possibility that within the diversity of the student body, some racial or ethnic groups may have been experiencing more equitable educational outcomes than others.

However, it is possible that through a process of inquiry, a diversity-minded individual such as this dean can learn to think from the perspective of equity. As it happens, this individual's cognitive frame evidenced a shift toward equity. In addition, members of the evidence teams whose dominant cognitive frame was diversity initially failed to see the need for disaggregating the data, a necessary condition for double-loop learning. Although disaggregating of data is not a guarantee of double-loop learning or equity thinking, it is a necessary step.

Other individuals were generally aware of unequal results, and the inquiry process was a catalyst for intensifying it and giving the individual the impetus to act more assertively to bring about change. For example, an individual, after having seen data on outcomes disaggregated by race and ethnicity, said, "I had always felt and had a pretty good sense of the situation of minority students, but then for the first time started looking at the data, and it was just overwhelming. So, [seeing the data] has really had a tremendous impact" (unpublished field notes, Center for Urban Education).

Although most institutions routinely disaggregate enrollment data, they rarely disaggregate data on more finely grained indicators of outcomes. When the evidence teams were asked to do this, these were some of the reactions we heard:

"We track financial aid, but we don't usually disaggregate it by ethnicity and types of awards."
"No one has ever asked us to disaggregate data by ethnicity and gender, and by program and academic preparation."
"I [chair of a humanities discipline] never asked [the institutional researcher] to disaggregate the data for my department. . . . I didn't have a reason."

In sum, disaggregated data serve as the medium through which individuals learn about unequal outcomes on behalf of their campuses. The way in which data are displayed and discussed can intensify learning, confirm or refute untested hypotheses, challenge preconceived ideas, motivate further inquiry, and provide the impetus for change.

Becoming Equity Minded. For practitioners to realize the enormity of the problem of unequal outcomes, they have to see hard evidence for themselves. This is accomplished by scrutinizing the data, asking questions that have suddenly come to mind, and discovering patterns of student conditions that had been concealed before the data were examined. Thus, to bring about new or intensified awareness of unequal results, evidence team members are directly involved in collecting student data, talking about the information, and using it to create equity measures and benchmarks to put into an institutional self-assessment tool known as the Equity Scorecard. The scorecard provides four concurrent perspectives on institutional performance in terms of equity in educational outcomes: access, retention, institutional receptivity, and excellence. The responsibility of the evidence teams was to create indicators of equity for each of the four perspectives. (The measures are available at http://www.usc.edu/dept/education/CUE/projects/ds/diversityscorecard.html.)

Typically institutional researchers are responsible for gathering and analyzing data, and their findings are disseminated primarily to administrators in written reports. In order to bring the members of the evidence teams in close proximity to the problem of unequal outcomes, they are assigned the role of researchers and have the responsibility for developing and interpreting the needed equity indicators. This heightens their awareness of the issues. Faculty members and others may be generally aware that there are disparities in educational outcomes, but persuading individuals to reflect on how their own practices may be contributing to the problem is another matter. They must learn to look at the particulars of the problem within their own context.

Shifting from Diversity and Deficit to an Equity Cognitive Frame. To illustrate the process of individuals' becoming more equity-minded, I introduce two individuals, whom I refer to as Carter and Stone, both actual members of evidence teams whose language during the course of the project changed noticeably from diversity and deficit to equity. I focus on these two individuals because their initial attitude toward the project was one of skepticism and lack of enthusiasm and because it was clear that for both of them, the concept of equity in educational outcomes was new and suspect. I will describe their cognitive frames before they saw any data disaggregated by race and ethnicity and after their team began to examine and talk about disaggregated data. These descriptions are based on field notes that describe what these individuals said in the context of their participation in their campus evidence team.

Carter is the dean that I referred to earlier whose initial reaction to the Equity Scorecard was that since the campus was so diverse, it would not be very useful and that he doubted what could be learned from the process of disaggregating data. Carter was a dean at a community college that was predominantly Hispanic and also had a large number of immigrants of all races and ethnicities from nations around the world. On our first meeting with this team, Carter, despite not having seen any data, was quick to say, "We are like the UN, so for us, there is not going to be any difference by ethnicity. In fact, by the very nature of the student population, what we are likely to find is that it is all bad" regardless of the students' ethnicity or racial background. The cognitive frames that are identifiable in this brief excerpt are diversity ("we are like the UN") and deficit ("the outcomes will be bad for all").

In subsequent meetings, when the team began to look at actual outcomes data that unequivocally showed Hispanics and blacks faring much worse than whites on just about every measure of educational outcomes, Carter's language began to change. Examining a printout showing grades earned in math courses broken down by race and ethnicity and seeing dramatic differences, he said, "I just think that there's going to be some nonpedagogical explanation, a racist explanation for lack of a better term." On the same day as he looked at data on student performance in gateway courses into the majors, he suddenly exclaimed, "Goddamit! Look at Business. There is a much higher success rate for whites than for the other groups. I bet that the reason for this is that some professors encourage particular students [high-achieving white immigrant ethnic groups] to take their course sections and give them better grades."

The point in this brief example is not whether this individual was right or wrong in attributing the inequalities he was seeing for the first time to racism. What matters is that Carter, on becoming aware of unequal outcomes, began to see the problem in ways that he had not previously considered. Rather than talking about diversity or suggesting that the differences in outcomes were a reflection of student deficits, he was considering the possibility that differences in outcomes might be attributable to individuals' unconscious practices or to institutional practices that unintentionally create circumstances that result in inequalities.

Like Carter, Stone is also in a college that is predominantly Hispanic and black, except that it is a four-year college. Before seeing data disaggregated by race and ethnicity, Stone's cognitive frame was clearly identifiable as diversity and deficit. At the outset of the project, he protested that "the Equity Scorecard focuses on remediating wrongs instead of celebrating differences." He said he would much rather "focus on how diversity is encouraged, celebrated, and welcomed" (diversity cognitive frame). At another meeting but before any data had been reviewed, he expressed a concern about the "low enrollment of Asians and whites among the first-time freshmen" and said that maybe they should be more concerned "with the dynamic of white flight" rather than with equity in outcomes (deficit cognitive frame). While this individual exhibited both diversity and deficit thinking, it was clear that deficit was his dominant cognitive frame. For example, on seeing data that Hispanics were graduating at a higher rate than whites, he commented that this was an "atypical" finding because it went against his expectation that Hispanics would do less well than whites.

After several months, this team finally began to look at disaggregated data, and once they did, Stone's language changed noticeably. For example, in looking at data that showed large gaps in the outcomes for African American students in mathematics, he said to the others on the team, "I am profoundly affected by the performance of African Americans." Had this statement been made by someone who had been identified as having an equity cognitive frame, it would not have attracted our attention. However, since up to this point Carter had been resistant to the equity-oriented aspects of the project and on different occasions had made comments that reflected a deficit perspective, being "profoundly" affected represented a departure from his usual way of thinking. I am not suggesting that simply because Stone admitted to being "profoundly affected by the performance of African Americans," he had experienced a sudden and dramatic shift in cognitive frames. Rather, his statement hinted at a possible change that we should watch for.

Indeed, subsequent statements demonstrated that he was undergoing a cognitive shift. For example, when one of his colleagues on the team mentioned how much had been learned by disaggregating data by race and ethnicity, Stone experienced an Aha! moment. He suddenly realized that the collaborative process of examining data served the purpose of "raising consciousness about disparities among different groups." "We almost do a disservice by not looking at equity as a focal point," he said. At another meeting, he spoke about the results of a faculty survey: "We conducted a faculty survey, and one item that was rated very high was the potential of our students." "But in conversations with faculty," it was disturbing for him to discover that despite espousing a belief in the students' potential, "they disparage their academic quality."

After this team began to examine data disaggregated by race and ethnicity and started discussing the clear-cut patterns of inequality that were revealed, Stone's language shifted from diversity and deficit toward equity. The language of deficit that had been prevalent in the first year of the project was gradually replaced by discourse that reflected a growing awareness of racism and inconsistencies in what faculty espouse at an abstract level as opposed to their actual perceptions when they speak about students from particular groups.

Do these brief illustrations suggest that individuals who reflected changes in their language and interpretations become equity minded? That is, do these subtle changes in language indicate that these individuals had changed and therefore were more likely to examine their own practices? Were they now ready to spearhead change within their own institutions? At this juncture in our work, it is premature to suggest that the learning evidenced in the shifts in interpretation will systematically translate into significant and large-scale changes. In addition, I cannot rule out that Carter and Stone will not revert to diversity or deficit thinking. Ultimately what is important is whether individuals like Carter and Stone consistently act from an equity frame of mind so that it spreads throughout the institution and becomes a shared way of thinking and acting. It would be foolhardy for me to assert that this goal has been achieved. Nevertheless, our work underscores that in order to move toward the reversal of unequal higher educational outcomes, individuals who occupy positions of power and authority, like Carter and Stone, or like me and the other authors of this volume, we all need to learn to think from the standpoint of equity. Unless that happens, we are not likely to even get started.

Conclusion

After four years of listening to and interpreting the conversations of the individuals who form the teams in the Equity Scorecard project, I believe that organizational learning, at the local level, by individuals who are closest to the problem may have a greater impact in reversing inequality in higher education than the numerous diversity-oriented interventions developed throughout the 1980s and 1990s. The illustrations I have shared provide a glimpse into the power of organizational learning to bring about changes in the cognitive frames of individuals. In essence, "the knowledge production itself may become the form of mobilization" that induces individuals to make the cognitive shift (Gaventa and Cornwall, 2001, p. 76) that leads to change from within the self outward to the institution.

References

Argyris, C. "Teaching Smart People How to Learn." *Reflections*, 1991, 4(2), 4–15.

Argyris, C. "Good Communication That Blocks Learning." In C. Argyris (ed.), *On Organizational Learning*. Boston: Harvard Business Review Press, 1994.

Argyris, C., and Schön, D. A. *Organizational Learning II: Theory, Method, and Practice.* Reading, Mass.: Addison-Wesley, 1996.

Bauman, G. L. "Developing a Culture of Evidence: Using Institutional Data to Identify Inequitable Educational Outcomes." Unpublished doctoral dissertation, University of Southern California, 2002.

Bensimon, E., and Neumann, A. *Redesigning Collegiate Leadership*. Baltimore, Md.: Johns Hopkins University Press, 1993.

Bensimon, E. M. "The Meaning of 'Good Presidential Leadership': A Frame Analysis." *Review of Higher Education*, 1989, 12(2), 107–123.

Bensimon, E. M. "Viewing the Presidency: Perceptual Congruence Between Presidents and Leaders on Their Campuses." *Leadership Quarterly*, 1990, 1(2), 71–90.

Bensimon, E. M. "The Diversity Scorecard: A Learning Approach to Institutional Change." *Change*, 2004, 36(1), 45–52.

Bensimon, E. M. *Equality in Fact, Equality in Results: A Matter of Institutional Accountability*. Washington D.C.: American Council on Education, 2005.

Bensimon, E. M., Hao, L., and Bustillos, L. T. "Measuring the State of Equity in Higher Education." In P. Gandara, G. Orfield, and C. Horn (eds.), Leveraging Promise and Expanding Opportunity in Higher Education. Albany: State University of New York Press, forthcoming.

Bensimon, E. M., Polkinghorne, D. E., Bauman, G. L., and Vallejo, E. "Research That Makes a Difference." *Journal of Higher Education*, 2004, 75(1), 104–126.

Coburn, C. E. "Rethinking Scale: Moving Beyond Numbers to Deep and Lasting Change." *Educational Researcher*, 2003, 32(6), 3–12.

Gaventa, J., and Cornwall, A. "Power and Knowledge." In P. Reason and H. Bradbury (eds.), *Handbook of Action Research*. Thousand Oaks, Calif.: Sage, 2001.

Grutter v. Bollinger, 539 U.S. 306, 2003.

Huber, G. P. "Organizational Learning: The Contributing Processes and the Literatures." *Organization Science*, 1991, 2(1), 88–115.

Kezar, A., Glenn, W., Lester, J., and Nakamoto, J. *Institutional Contexts and Equitable Educational Outcomes: Empowered to Learn*. University of Southern California: Center for Urban Education, 2004.

Kim, D. "The Link Between Individual and Organizational Learning." *Sloan Management Review*, 1993, *35*(1), 37–50.

Neumann, A. "Strategic Leadership: The Changing Orientations of College Presidents." *Review of Higher Education*, 1989, *12*(2), 137–151.

Neumann, A., and Bensimon, E. M. "Constructing the Presidency: College Presidents' Images of Their Leadership Roles, a Comparative Study." *Journal of Higher Education*, 1990, *61*(6), 678–701.

Pollock, M. "How the Question We Ask Most About Race in Education Is the Very Question We Most Suppress." *Educational Researcher*, 2001, *30*(9), 2–12.

Stanton-Salazar, R. *Manufacturing Hope and Despair: The School and Kin Support Networks of U.S.-Mexican Youth.* New York: Teachers College Press, 2001.

ESTELA MARA BENSIMON is a professor of higher education and the director of the Center for Urban Education in the Rossier School of Education at the University of Southern California.

9

Organizational learning, along with a framework for diversity, is an effective approach for campuses seeking sustained institutional change with regard to diversity.

Organizational Learning: A Tool for Diversity and Institutional Effectiveness

Daryl G. Smith, Sharon Parker

Colleges and Universities have been engaging in efforts related to diversity for decades. While the focus on diversity has waxed and waned during this period, the current demographic shifts in the country have created perhaps one of the most compelling times to engage diversity issues. The combination of these profound demographic changes and the stark socioeconomic and racial gaps that continue to exist in U.S. society and higher education signify a fast increasing educational and career readiness gap between haves and have-nots. This is especially troubling in the light of the increasing demands for education and for competency.

Despite much rhetoric to the contrary, many institutions are hard-pressed to say how, and whether, progress on diversity is being made. Often when asked about progress, campus leaders respond with anecdotes and a list of programs. Indeed, as the discourse on diversity has increased, the list of programs has also increased. One leader in the field has suggested that this tendency toward "projectitis"—equating diversity progress with diversity activity—is a real problem (Shireman, 2003). As programs and activities increase, it has become clear that institutional capacity to monitor institutional progress has not increased. Moreover, as campuses, particularly in states like California, become more racially and ethnically diverse at the undergraduate level, they are likely to think that they are succeeding at diversity simply by looking at the demographics of that population. This chapter proposes that using the approach of organizational learning along with a framework for diversity is an effective approach for campuses seeking sustained institutional change with regard to diversity.

The Need for a New Approach

In recent studies of the lack of progress on diversity issues, a number of patterns have emerged that are common among institutions engaged in diversity work throughout the country. These patterns are highly relevant because they underscore some of the barriers to effective change. First, few campuses have adequate information about the institutional impact of their diversity work and about measurable progress toward their espoused goals. Rather, campus reviews of diversity efforts often consist of information on specific program activities and individuals or groups that have benefited from such programs. Without usable data and analytical reporting, it is difficult, even impossible, to determine whether any progress has been made concerning issues such as access and success for underrepresented populations or institutional changes required to build capacity for diversity. Second, campuses tend not to be aware of the connection between their programs and institutional goals for diversity. Although diversity efforts produce many worthwhile programs, these may or may not facilitate the achievement of specific institutional goals, such as student success. Consequently, on campuses across the country, diversity projects have come to be substituted for diversity progress. Third, it has become clear that with all the demands on campus leaders, only those engaged in the day-to-day work of diversity efforts remain focused on diversity results. Yet campus progress on diversity rests on many other key people in an institution, including senior leadership. Fourth, it appears that evaluation of diversity efforts relies on traditional institutional approaches that reduce it to a pro forma procedure whose primary purpose is to satisfy an imposed requirement by a foundation, for example. In addition, this approach does not provide opportunities for corrective actions during the course of implementation.

These patterns call for a new approach to increase campus capacity to evaluate the effectiveness of its diversity work in making progress toward its institutional goals. Increasingly organizational learning is emerging as a means of addressing a variety of issues in numerous contexts (Hernandez and Visher, 2001). Other foundations have used an information-based approach to evaluation (W. K. Kellogg, 1998), and regional accreditation organizations have been introducing an organizational learning model for quality improvement (Western Association of Schools and Colleges [WASC], 2002). Many such organizations are now engaged in an effort to see if, and how, organizational learning increases campus capacity to evaluate progress toward important institutional goals and encourages strategic decision making.

Learning from other evaluations of diversity work nationally (Musil and others, 1999; Nettles and others, 2002; Smith and others, 2000), the work of other philanthropic organizations (Pew Charitable Trusts, 2001; Preskill and Torres, 1999; W. K. Kellogg Foundation, 1998), and assessments of its own prior diversity grants (Smith, 1997), the James Irvine Foundation incorporated an organizational learning approach into its evaluation strategies. Its entire grant-making process for the Campus Diversity Initiative (CDI) was designed to include an organizational learning approach to its work with twenty-eight independent colleges and universities in California since 2000. Some of the observations and tools developed for that project are used as the basis for this chapter. (They are described at http://www.aacu.org/irvinediveval and www.irvine.org.)

The CDI has involved twenty-eight independent colleges and universities in California in addressing diversity. The goals are to increase the success of historically underrepresented students in higher education (African American, Latino, and Native American students, and low-income students of all backgrounds) and to develop institutional capacity to prepare all college students for participation and leadership in a diverse society. The CDI was designed to (1) strengthen the impact of campus diversity efforts, (2) increase institutional ability to monitor progress on diversity using a collaborative organizational learning framework, and (3) contribute to the knowledge base in the field. To support these objectives, the CDI Evaluation Project was formed as a collaboration between the Claremont Graduate University and the Association of American Colleges and Universities to assist the campuses in their evaluation work, facilitate cross-campus information sharing, and provide references to evaluation materials (for example, http://www.aacu.org/irvinediveval). The project codirectors are Daryl G. Smith, Sharon Parker, and Alma Clayton-Pedersen.

Rationale for Linking Organizational Learning and Diversity

In theory, organizational learning seems to be particularly well suited to colleges and universities that are dealing with demographic and other changes (Bensimon, Polkington, Bauman, and Vallejo, 2004; Boyce, 2003; Eckel, Green, and Hill, 2001). They are not hierarchical entities in which change can easily be mandated. Hiring issues, curricular change, and many other aspects of diversity efforts rest with a broad and disparate group of individuals on a campus. In addition, the highly decentralized nature of campus decision making means that collective efforts, rather than simply administrative decisions, are required. Moreover, in contrast to the language typically associated with outcomes assessment or evaluation, organizational learning does not necessarily imply that only highly specialized experts can engage in the evaluation process. Organizational learning asks whether thoughtful people mindful of the institutional context and using relevant and available information can facilitate needed change. Because diversity efforts inevitably require a broad range of constituents, a process that allows, indeed, requires, a broad range of constituent participation is well suited to diversity.

Furthermore, unlike compliance reporting models to various outside agencies (including traditional accreditation and funding agencies) that look at successful components of programmatic initiatives on completion, organizational learning is focused on the process of the effort and takes action to ensure progress toward success by making changes or corrections as necessary. This process shifts the focus to the effectiveness of the effort to achieve the desired outcome. Institutions continually engaged in a cross-institutional analysis of progress, or its absence, understand how and where the process needs correction to ensure successful attainment of goals. Again, given the traditional campus emphasis on diversity programs and activities, organizational learning can shift the diversity discussion to institutional-level goals and institutional success in achieving those goals.

For diversity initiatives, organizational learning has the potential to lead to greater effectiveness because it relates to the core work of the institution. Based on analysis of collected institutional data, organizational learning holds the promise of being more informative and usable. It encourages the use of structures in which members of the campus community can honestly reflect on successes and failures and take ownership of the process and the results. It involves a broad representation of cross-institutional decision makers. It is not a process imposed from the outside but takes into consideration both internal and external community influences. Finally, it builds on the academic discourse of educational effectiveness that is already familiar to institutional leaders. In the end, it is also likely to provide better information on which to judge the overall impact of efforts. At a conceptual level, using organizational learning in learning organizations seems to make sense. Can one differ with the notion that "intentionality and thoughtfulness should be the hallmarks of change in the academy" (Eckel, Green, and Hill, 2001)?

Building Institutional Capacity for Organizational Learning and Diversity

As a result of the James Irvine Foundation CDI effort, we now have a manageable and coherent approach to diversity work in higher education that includes a set of principles, a framework for organizing the effort, and a set of indicators that guide the collection and analysis of data. Each of these components forms a conceptual structure that creates organizational learning. While this structure has emerged from the CDI Evaluation Project work with twenty-eight private campuses, it can be generalized for many different campuses seriously committed to effective institutional change on issues of diversity.

To begin, campus applicants for CDI funds were engaged in a three-step process. We realized that campuses had to have some initial conditions in place in order to be ready to learn. First, colleges and universities were asked to assess the status of diversity on their campus in the context of their own history and mission. Only when the campus had identified its greatest areas of need was a formal proposal requested. Next, each campus developed a diversity evaluation plan that included the means by which to address the fundamental question: How can we know if we are making progress? This way of approaching the question is significant because the question does not emphasize the usual language of evaluation but rather asks educated people in an institutional context to determine how they might come to know whether they are making progress on such matters as student success, faculty hiring, and curriculum change. Finally, all grantee institutions were requested to submit an interim report every six months. The reports were intended to be learning organization tools drawing on available data, as well as updates on the formative process of campus diversity work. For any campus interested in providing a strategic approach to diversity, these three steps are emerging as essential:

1. Establishing the history and status of diversity, including a set of baseline data
2. Developing a plan for monitoring progress
3. Developing an ongoing process for information collection and a time and place to discuss progress and make necessary changes

Moreover, the documents developed for each of these stages have proven essential in maintaining continuity of effort and institutional memory over time. In effect, by gathering manageable and relevant institutional information about the progress of the campus toward its goals and by supporting a process by which campuses would monitor and discuss progress, information becomes available that is centrally relevant to the campus community (as well as any outside funders or constituencies).

The approach to the evaluation project included a number of principles that were continually emphasized and lead to learning. These principles focus on developing information that is manageable, relevant to the needs of the particular institution, its mission and culture, and that generates an ongoing process (see Exhibit 9.1). The principles have great relevance for campuses attempting to approach diversity efforts using organizational learning.

The principles include making sure that campuses are focusing on institutional goals and not simply program activities. For example, campuses are encouraged to examine all related retention efforts in their monitoring process, not simply a single retention program or activity. This approach is best understood when campuses keep in mind that retention is the result of universitywide practices, not just the responsibility of designated support programs.

Exhibit 9.1. Campus Diversity Initiative Project Principles

- Approaches evaluation from an organizational learning point of view
- Manageable for campus and capable of being maintained
- Monitors key goals and elements of proposal
- Focuses on institutional issues/change, not simply project-specific issues
- Reveals success and problems along the way in both results and processes
- Guides the six month reports to the Foundation
- Takes into account:
  - Institutional differences and stages with respect to diversity
  - That institutions vary in mission, needs, goals and culture
  - That strategies, goals and emphasis differ
  - The possibility of taking some risks and learning from them
  - Differences within institutions (disaggregation of information)
- Encourages institutional sharing
- Uses the evaluation liaison and evaluation resource team in an advisory capacity

Perhaps more important to the process of encouraging learning is a framework. Without a structure by which the conversations can be defined and framed, conversations on diversity are likely to be frustrating and useless. Discussions of diversity on college campuses typically occur in many locations and from different perspectives. For campus leadership, the focus may be on noting progress of changes in demographic representation. For others, the focus of attention may be the many areas in which institutional capacity to address diversity has not changed. Conversations are thus neither focused nor effective in looking at diversity from a strategic point of view. Our framework has emerged from the work on diversity nationally. Overall, it provides a useful way of both describing where institutions engage diversity and capturing the key elements of diversity efforts. The framework also suggests the important interrelationships among the different dimensions of diversity.

The central goals of many diversity initiatives have been relatively clear: to increase access and success of historically and economically disadvantaged students and to increase institutional capacity to address diversity effectively. In the end, although there is considerable variation in institutional context and emphasis, there is also considerable overlap in campus goals and strategies. These approaches to goals and strategies have been organized using a framework for diversity that falls within four dimensions (Smith, 1999): access and success of underrepresented students, campus climate and intergroup relations, education and scholarship, and institutional viability (see Figure 9.1).

As part of the framework, a set of indicators evolved from work with campuses on diversity and institutional change. For example, key indicators include persistence and retention data disaggregated by race, ethnicity, and gender and, where possible, socioeconomic status. Some of the ways

Figure 9.1. Framework for Diversity

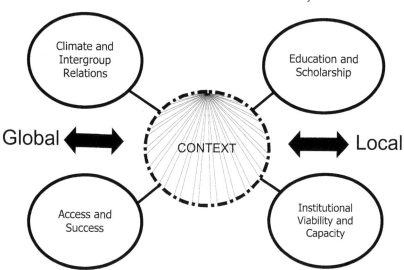

that the framework applies to campuses and the relevant indicators that can be used to monitor campus efforts are described in the following sections. Figure 9.2 shows the indicators of access and success.

Many campuses are still working on access at the undergraduate or graduate level to increase the racial/ethnic diversity present in their student bodies through outreach, partnerships, summer programs, and admissions approaches. For example, there are campuses that have been very successful with Latino students but less successful with African American students. Furthermore, campuses are now acknowledging the need to address institutional responsibility for continuing gaps in achievement and success of specific populations. It is especially important in this regard that some campuses have moved beyond basic indicators of success (graduation, retention, grade point average) and are focused on whether students from underrepresented racial and ethnic groups are thriving at the institution— that is achieving honors, graduating in science and math fields, or generally engaged on campus. While virtually all campuses remain focused on the access and success of historically underrepresented populations (African Americans, Latinos, American Indians), more and more campuses are also engaging the experiences of different Asian American populations, such as Filipino students, as well as first-generation students from lower economic backgrounds. Focusing on groups that have been historically significant while paying attention to populations that are increasing in California is an important development in diversity initiatives.

Figure 9.2. Indicators of Access and Success

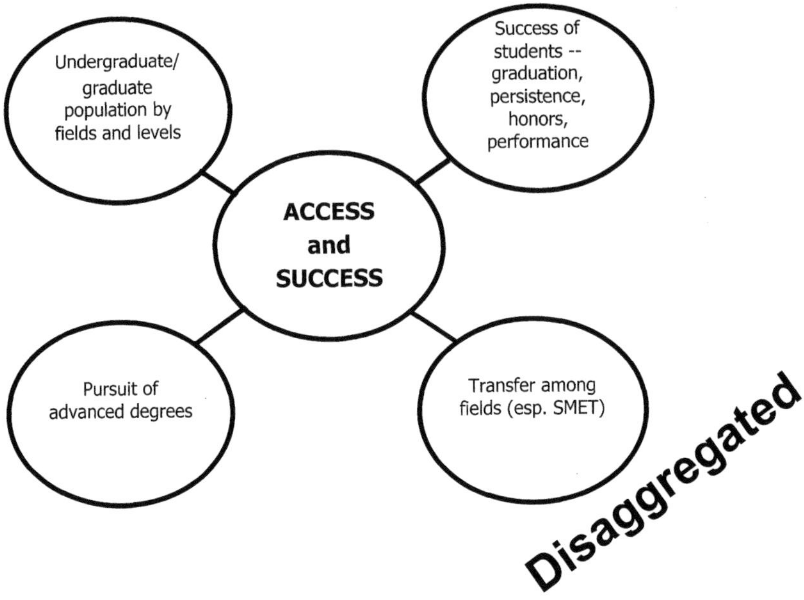

Discussion and Reflection

The CDI structured the reflection and discussion about campus progress using six-month interim reports to the foundation. What has emerged most clearly is the necessity for campuses to have a highly structured mechanism to create opportunities to review data and link the data to relevant decision making. The process of reporting every six months created the opportunity for campuses to collect and review data and other information on the indicators and provided a mechanism to institute corrective actions as needed. An overarching intent of this process has been to prompt campuses to look holistically and reflectively at their progress toward the institutional goals they articulated and to look longitudinally at disaggregated data on a regular basis.

One of the early observations of this process is that developing the capacity to generate, present, and use data for institutional purposes does not always come easily. The tendency for staff who are already busy, and often overburdened, is to prepare and submit interim reports in a compliance mode rather than using them to facilitate campus learning. Central to whether this reporting process is handled as a learning opportunity or a compliance task is how much the institutional culture facilitates or impedes the use and sharing of data, as well as how the role of the institutional research officer is defined. Encouraging the use of these reports on campus has required continued prompting. In a context in which such reports are not required, it is clear that some other structure, probably initiated by institutional leaders, will be necessary if the campus is to make time for reflection on information and formulation of decisions regarding implementation adjustments. It is clear that even when a campus has data, this information is not routinely used to monitor progress or make strategic decisions or changes. Interim reports provide an opportunity for this to occur. A key issue for campuses in general is how to make the process of data collection and analysis a part of institutional practice. If the diversity framework and indicators are used by campus leadership to provide an audit of campus progress, in much the same way that a financial audit provides a regular glimpse of financial progress and health, campuses would make more sustainable efforts to institutional change. With the progression of the CDI, a number of other patterns have emerged with potential significance for both organizational learning and diversity efforts.

Institutional Framework. Using an institutional framework for monitoring diversity is very important. A framework that is established at the beginning of the diversity initiative and is manageable becomes a model to facilitate discussion and monitor change in a focused and manageable way. It provides an institutional map that guides leaders toward institutional goals and prevents side excursions from supplanting those goals. Moreover, it enables leaders to see how their programs contribute toward reaching the institutional goal rather than being isolated activities. Rather than getting paralyzed by discussions on the definition of diversity, for example, this framework has proven useful in capturing both diversity work and its relevant indicators.

Using Data. Campuses, almost no matter what their size, are complex and highly decentralized entities. While we might wish otherwise, they have little experience in the use of data to inform decisions, and relevant data are not as accessible as one might think. Obvious data such as longitudinal information on graduation and retention disaggregated by race and ethnicity often have to be developed. While a research culture encourages transparency of data and information in the academic setting, such information can be quite difficult at the institutional level. Information often has institutional and political significance that needs to be taken into consideration. Because the sharing of information may generate controversy for the leadership or the reputation of the institution, it is hard to overcome the desire to want to make the campus look good or avoid making information too public. This is particularly true for a context in which diversity has been the object of intense political and legal challenges. Moreover, the wide range of opinions on campuses and the diffusion of leadership mean that conversations about diversity can be contentious and difficult to engage. Nonetheless, the use of basic, disaggregated institutional data is fundamental to monitoring and discussing progress. Two elements appear critical. First, creating a manageable and agreed-on framework organizes the effort and creates the potential for continuity over time. Second, the campus needs to designate a regular time and place for discussion of results.

Parallel Initiatives. The relationship between organizational learning in colleges and universities and the learning and research orientation of higher education is not a simple one. What might seem to be a sensible and obvious process interrupts typical campus patterns at almost every point. From bringing together campus constituents across institutional boundaries and accessing campus information data systems to obtain usable information, the process of using an organizational learning approach for evaluation has challenged many campuses. At the same time, diversity work also interrupts the usual—whether in considering admissions standards, faculty hiring processes, or definitions of good practice, for example. Thus, while having the potential to facilitate change, the combination of two intense processes—diversity work and organizational learning—often runs on parallel courses. The need to continually encourage campuses to be intentional about linking both efforts is one of the most important lessons that has emerged from the project.

Leadership. Leadership at many levels of the institution is another important element for success. However, because diversity efforts are not deeply embedded in the institutional culture and practice, leaders at all levels have to be reminded to use the organizational learning approach to keep both diversity and evaluation at the center of institutional discourse. A key factor in the success of institutional efforts and in keeping the senior leadership focused on progress is the presence of a diversity coordinator or director who understands the significance of organizational learning to changing institutional culture and practice with respect to diversity. Leadership can ensure that diversity and organizational learning do not become parallel initiatives.

Link to Mission and Culture. Because there is an important relationship between organizational culture and diversity work (Ibarra, 2000; Kezar and Eckel, 2002; Aleman and Salkever, 2003), linking diversity initiatives to institutional mission and overall educational effectiveness is essential for campuses to reach their institutional goals. Most campuses have not had much experience in using evaluation to serve institutional purposes or for learning from their successes and failures. Not only do some campus cultures and missions facilitate diversity work, some also facilitate the use of evidence in promoting change. For example, institutions with social justice missions tend to address diversity issues directly. Indeed, on campuses where diversity is not understood as central to mission, the use of organizational learning and an evaluation plan for institutional effectiveness may be critical to keep diversity from remaining at the margins. For example, all CDI institutions are being asked to develop evidence on student success, engagement, and learning. By disaggregating data, the campus is able to ask who is succeeding and how, thus linking the effectiveness discourse with diversity.

Organizational Learning as the Work of Individuals or Institutions. The literature on organizational learning uses language of the institution as the unit of analysis. Increasingly, there are those who suggest that organizational learning is the work of individuals who must be the focus. Conceptually, of course, institutions are made up of individuals who do the work of the campus, introduce change, challenge norms, and so forth. However, individuals and teams work in a context that either enhances or complicates organizational learning and diversity. The CDI Evaluation Project has highlighted a number of factors that strongly influence the effectiveness of individual or team efforts and the ultimate impact these efforts have on institutional indicators. These include the potentially dramatic turnover in personnel, the culture of the institution in relation to the use of data, the role of senior leadership at all levels that either foster and encourage organizational learning or discourage it, the presence of effective and capable institutional researchers, and the purpose of the institution.

Continuity. It takes time for cross-institutional teams that come together to address diversity issues to build manageable and beneficial collaborations. Consequently, the issues of turnover and continuity at all levels of campus diversity efforts remain a powerful factor. It has been common to have turnover of half of the key participants in the diversity work throughout the institution. Overcoming the impact of transitions takes intentionality. That is, for new participants to work effectively with the remaining leadership and be aware of past work and organizational history, there needs to be an intentional process for their inclusion. Good communication is an important element of this process but is not always easy to achieve. How to respond appropriately to these issues in the context of each institution is important. Use of the key documents developed for the diversity initiative (institutional overview, proposal, evaluation plan, and interim reports) has proven to be an important strategy for maintaining continuity through transition.

Intentionality. The notion of intentionality is a necessary component of organizational learning and often requires interrupting the usual, that is, thoughtful action applied in a purposeful manner. Consequently, while it seems to be true that organizational learning makes sense and fits the culture of higher education, it also seems to be true that the process of building an evidence-based context for change means interrupting the usual institutional practices and norms at every step. Similarly, many campuses, as well as organizations outside higher education, fail to fully grasp the complexity of issues involved in harnessing the benefits that diversity can lend to achieving institutional goals. Moreover, the process of institutionalizing diversity is so complex (involving multiple stakeholders with varying levels of investment and authority, varying resources, intense emotions, and controversial issues) that business as usual will not suffice.

Conclusion

Higher education institutions that employ a learning organization evaluation approach have the opportunity to achieve their institutional diversity goals. The design of the approach outlined in this chapter is based on an assumption of intentionality and cross-institutional involvement that embeds diversity strategies and goals broadly and deeply to ensure long-term sustainability. The three-step process of institutional diversity assessment, evaluation, and monitoring plan and interim reports was developed to encourage campuses to look at themselves holistically and in context in order to promote intentionality in clarifying the goals and monitoring them over time. While it is likely that this organizational learning model can yield meaningful and sustainable progress on diversity, the supposition that organizational learning is a natural for higher education institutions is not necessarily true. At the same time, however, it seems to be the most likely process to keep an institution focused on monitoring progress toward its institutional diversity goals.

References

Aleman, A.M.M., and Salkever, K. "Mission, Multiculturalism, and the Liberal Arts College: A Qualitative Investigation." *Journal of Higher Education,* 2003, 74(5), 563–596.

Bensimon, E. M., Polkington, D. E., Bauman, G., and Vallejo, E. "Doing Research That Makes a Difference." *Journal of Higher Education,* 2004, 75(1), 104–126.

Boyce, M. E. "Organizational Learning Is Essential to Achieving and Sustaining Change in Higher Education." *Innovative Higher Education,* 2003, 28(2), 119–136.

Eckel, P., Green, M., and Hill, B. *On Change V: Riding the Wings of Change: Insights from Transforming Institutions.* Washington, D.C.: American Council on Education, 2001.

Hernandez, G., and Visher, M. *Creating a Culture of Inquiry: A James Irvine Foundation Report.* San Francisco: James Irvine Foundation, 2001.

Ibarra, R. A. *Beyond Affirmative Action: Reframing the Context of Higher Education.* Madison: University of Wisconsin Press, 2000.

Kezar, A., and Eckel, P. "The Effect of Institutional Culture on Change Strategies in Higher Education." *Journal of Higher Education,* 2002, 73(4), 435–460.

Musil, C. M., and others. *To Form a More Perfect Union: Campus Diversity Initiatives.* Washington, D.C.: Association of American Colleges and Universities, 1999.

Nettles, M., and others. *Assessing Diversity on College and University Campuses.* Washington, D.C.: Association of American Colleges and Universities, 2002.

Pew Charitable Trusts. *Returning Results: Planning and Evaluation at the Pew Charitable Trusts.* Philadelphia: Author, 2001.

Preskill, H., and Torres, R. T. *Inquiry for Learning in Organizations.* Thousand Oaks, Calif.: Sage, 1999.

Shireman, R. "Ten Questions College Officials Should Ask About Diversity." *Chronicle Review,* Aug. 15, 2003. http://chronicle.com/prm/weekly/v49/i49/49b01001.htm.

Smith, D. G. *Evaluation Report: To the James Irvine Foundation on the Campus Diversity Initiative.* San Francisco: James Irvine Foundation, 1997.

Smith, D. G. "Strategic Evaluation: An Imperative for the Future of Campus Diversity." In M. Cross and others (eds.), *Diversity and Unity: The Role of Higher Education in Building Democracy.* Capetown, South Africa: Maskew MillerLongman, 1999.

Smith, D. G. *The James Irvine Campus Diversity Initiative: Current Status, Anticipating the Future*, 2004. http://www.irvine.org/publications/by_topic/education.shtml.

Smith, D. G., and others. *A Diversity Research Agenda*. Washington, D.C.: American Association of Schools and Colleges, 2000.

WASC. *A Guide to Using Evidence in the Accreditation Process*. Oakland, Calif.: Author, 2002.

W. K. Kellogg Foundation. *Evaluation Handbook*. Battle Creek, Mich.: W. K. Kellogg Foundation, 1998.

DARYL G. SMITH is professor of education and psychology at the Claremont Graduate University in Claremont, California.

SHARON PARKER is a visiting faculty member at the Claremont Graduate University in Claremont, California, and a resource faculty member at Evergreen State College in Olympia, Washington.

INDEX

Back Issue/Subscription Order Form

Copy or detach and send to:

Jossey-Bass, A Wiley Company, 989 Market Street, San Francisco CA 94103-1741

Call or fax toll-free: Phone 888-378-2537 6:30AM – 3PM PST; Fax 888-481-2665

Back Issues: Please send me the following issues at $29 each
(Important: please include series initials and issue number, such as HE114.)

_____

_____

_____

$ _____   Total for single issues

$ _____   SHIPPING CHARGES: SURFACE   Domestic   Canadian
                                   First Item $5.00 $6.00
                                   Each Add'l Item $3.00 $1.50
                 For next-day and second-day delivery rates, call the number listed above.

Subscriptions: Please __start __renew my subscription to *New Directions for Higher Education* for the year 2____at the following rate:

U.S.	__Individual $80	__Institutional $170
Canada	__Individual $80	__Institutional $210
All Others	__Individual $104	__Institutional $244

**For more information about online subscriptions visit
www.interscience.wiley.com**

$ _____   Total single issues and subscriptions (Add appropriate sales tax for your state for single issue orders. No sales tax for U.S. subscriptions. Canadian residents, add GST for subscriptions and single issues.)

__Payment enclosed (U.S. check or money order only)
__VISA __MC __AmEx #_____ Exp. Date _____

Signature _____ Day Phone _____
__ Bill Me (U.S. institutional orders only. Purchase order required.)

Purchase order # _____
                 Federal Tax ID13559302   GST 89102 8052

Name _____

Address _____

_____

Phone _____ E-mail _____

For more information about Jossey-Bass, visit our Web site at **www.josseybass.com**

NEW DIRECTIONS FOR HIGHER EDUCATION IS NOW AVAILABLE ONLINE AT WILEY INTERSCIENCE

What is Wiley InterScience?

Wiley InterScience is the dynamic online content service from John Wiley & Sons delivering the full text of over 300 leading scientific, technical, medical, and professional journals, plus major reference works, the acclaimed *Current Protocols* laboratory manuals, and even the full text of select Wiley print books online.

What are some special features of Wiley InterScience?

Wiley InterScience Alerts is a service that delivers table of contents via e-mail for any journal available on Wiley InterScience as soon as a new issue is published online.
Early View is Wiley's exclusive service presenting individual articles online as soon as they are ready, even before the release of the compiled print issue. These articles are complete, peer-reviewed, and citable.
CrossRef is the innovative multi-publisher reference linking system enabling readers to move seamlessly from a reference in a journal article to the cited publication, typically located on a different server and published by a different publisher.

How can I access Wiley InterScience?

Visit http://www.interscience.wiley.com

Guest Users can browse Wiley InterScience for unrestricted access to journal Tables of Contents and Article Abstracts, or use the powerful search engine.
Registered Users are provided with a *Personal Home Page* to store and manage customized alerts, searches, and links to favorite journals and articles. Additionally, Registered Users can view free Online Sample Issues and preview selected material from major reference works.
Licensed Customers are entitled to access full-text journal articles in PDF, with select journals also offering full-text HTML.

How do I become an Authorized User?

Authorized Users are individuals authorized by a paying Customer to have access to the journals in Wiley InterScience. For example, a university that subscribes to Wiley journals is considered to be the Customer. Faculty, staff and students authorized by the university to have access to those journals in Wiley InterScience are Authorized Users. Users should contact their Library for information on which Wiley journals they have access to in Wiley InterScience.

ASK YOUR INSTITUTION ABOUT WILEY INTERSCIENCE TODAY!

Made in the USA
Lexington, KY
24 August 2010